Dr Bunty Avieson is a journalist, author and academic. She has published three novels, a novella and a travel memoir. Her books have been translated into Japanese, German and Thai, and she is the winner of two Ned Kelly Awards for crime writing. She worked for 20 years as a journalist and feature writer on newspapers and magazines in Australia, Great Britain and Asia. In the 1990s she was editor of *Woman's Day* and editorial director of *New Idea*. She is currently a lecturer in the Department of Media and Communications at the University of Sydney.

Also by Bunty Avieson

Fiction

Once You Know

The Wrong Door

The Affair

Apartment 255

Non-Fiction

A Baby in a Backpack to Bhutan

THE Dragon's Voice

How Modern Media Found Bhutan

BUNTY AVIESON

UQP

First published 2013 by Bhutan Observer Pvt Ltd as *The Dragon Finds Its Voice*
This updated edition published 2015 by University of Queensland Press
PO Box 6042, St Lucia, Queensland 4067 Australia

www.uqp.com.au
uqp@uqp.uq.edu.au

Cover design by Christabella Designs
All photographs in picture section by Mal Watson unless otherwise stated
Author photograph by Kathryn Avieson
Typeset in 11.5/16 pt Minion Pro by Post Pre-press Group, Brisbane
Printed in Australia by McPherson's Printing Group

Cataloguing-in-Publication Data
National Library of Australia

Creator: Avieson, Bunty, author.

Title: The dragon's voice : how modern media found Bhutan / Bunty Avieson.

ISBN 978 0 7022 53577 (pbk)
ISBN 978 0 7022 55038 (ePDF)
ISBN 978 0 7022 55045 (ePub)
ISBN 978 0 7022 55052 (Kindle)

Subjects: Press–Bhutan.
Journalism–Social aspects–Bhutan.
Journalism–Political aspects–Bhutan.
Bhutan in mass media.
Bhutan–Description and travel.
Bhutan–Social life and customs.

079.5498

University of Queensland Press uses papers that are natural, renewable and recyclable products
made from wood grown in sustainable forests. The logging and manufacturing processes
conform to the environmental regulations of the country of origin.

Contents

Just as Alice, when she first walked through the looking glass, found herself in a new and whimsical world, so we found ourselves as though caught up on some magic time machine, fitted fantastically with a reverse.

Lord Ronaldshay, Governor of Bengal, upon reaching Bhutan in 1921

The media are not just watchdogs of society, they are changing society itself. Media are constructing new realities and values.

Siok Sian Pek-Dorji, *Media Impact Study 2008*

PROLOGUE

Crowning a King

Bhutan's Dragon King takes the Raven Crown, a bird's head decorated with skulls, and holds it steady above his smoothly handsome 28-year-old son. It is a few seconds short of 8.31 am, on 6 November 2008, the eighth day of the ninth month of the Earth Male Rat Year, deemed by royal soothsayers to be highly auspicious. The air swirls about them, dense with incense. Bearing witness inside the small 13th-century chamber are 70 VVIPs (Very Very Important Persons) and members of Bhutan's extended royal family.

On the roof above, boy monks blow antique horns in a cacophony that bounces around the stone walls and soars over the country's capital, Thimphu.

Across the kingdom of 630,000 people, villagers crowd into homes lucky enough to have one of the country's 47,000 television sets, while some yak herders, high in rocky crags, listen to the radio commentary streaming live through their mobile phones. Introduced just four years ago, the mobile phone became an instant success, and now more than 250,000 Bhutanese own one – more than a third of the population. This ancient mystical ceremony is the country's first modern media event, and the latest technologies are taking it live to the most remote corners of the kingdom.

To the people of Bhutan, the coronation of this new young King marks the end of life as they have known it. In the past year, King Jigme Singye Wangchuck, known affectionately as the Fourth King, handed much of his power over to the first democratically elected government, and created the country's first constitution. Placing the crown on his son's head is his last, final duty.

After 30 years of rule, today he will withdraw from public life to spend his remaining years with his four wives, relaxing and meditating. Many Bhutanese cannot imagine life without their beloved Fourth King in charge, and some are in tears as they watch or listen to the ceremony. No longer will he make all the decisions for the country – there is a new government and a new King to do that – and for his loyal subjects the future looks frighteningly uncertain.

During his reign the Fourth King guided his tiny kingdom into the 21st century. The country is peaceful, more prosperous and better educated than when he took over in 1972 at the age of just 17. Bhutan has its own well-developed culture – utterly unique – and protects it fiercely. The Fourth King identified shortcomings in the Gross National Product measure of other countries, and instead created for his people the Buddhist-inspired concept of Gross National Happiness (GNH) as his country's measure of wealth, which has brought international curiosity and immense national pride.

By any measure the Fourth King has been a dynamic and successful ruler. His heir, King Jigme Khesar Namgyel Wangchuck, the fifth Druk Gyalpo (Dragon King), will face entirely different challenges. As he takes the throne, Bhutan is not only striding forward as a new democracy but also rocketing into the information age. Along with mobile phones, Bhutan is rolling out a broadband internet network and satellite television, thereby opening its doors to an outside world drunk on consumerism, celebrity culture and Western excesses. The noise is shrill and raucous as it seeps into this peaceful feudal country, where nearly 10 per cent of the population are monks and nuns.

The new monarch, who from today will be referred to as the Fifth King, is expected to lead his people through these modern challenges, while showing the same wisdom and compassion as his forefathers. He is expected to provide moral authority, yet remain above politics. While the Fourth King established the pillars of the new democracy, it will be the Fifth King who will shape a new role for the monarchy; lead his unworldly people into the future; and, most importantly, in this last bastion of Vajrayana Buddhism, take responsibility for the spiritual advancement of his people.

The Fifth King understands the sacredness of his position. The Bhutanese believe it is his karma to receive this legacy: it reflects spiritual attainments and connections from his previous lives. As a Buddhist King, he is a modern-day dharma protector, ensuring Buddhism is nurtured and allowed to flourish among his people. It is both a practical and an inspirational role, without Western equivalent. Bhutanese historian and author Tshering Tashi writes that the responsibility is so great that no ordinary person would want the role.

Despite its public transfer of power, the coronation is also a moment of quiet intimacy for father and son. The two men are close, often photographed holding hands. When the auspicious moment arrives, the Fourth King places the crown gently upon his son's head then steps away, leaving the new ruler alone on the throne. Other members of the royal family file up to pay homage, offering white scarves and a formal bow. First, the Queen Grandmother, stooped and serene, followed by the Fourth King's wives. They are four beautiful sisters who married the Fourth King in one big ceremony. Each lives in her own royal palace, and they have always been treated equally. To avoid upsetting this harmonious status quo, from this moment on they will all assume the title of Queen Mother.

They greet their new King in order of seniority, eldest to youngest. When it comes the turn of the third, the Fifth King's birth mother, she cannot resist reaching up to the throne and cupping her son's cheek in her palm. It is quickly over, an almost imperceptible gesture of tenderness and maternal pride, unnoticed by the VVIPs inside the chamber but broadcast live around the nation on BBS, the Bhutan Broadcasting Service. For villagers to see either of the Kings in living, breathing colour on a box inside the home is still a novelty. To be taken inside the private chamber of Tashichhodzong to see the whole royal family undergoing this ancient ritual is a jaw-dropping experience.

Outside, the international media shiver in a corner of the courtyard. It is quite a crowd: Reuters, Associated Press, British newspaper *The Independent*, Radio America, a US documentary team, *Vanity Fair*, *OK!* from Thailand and *Glamour* from Germany, Indian newspapers and television, Japanese television, *The Sydney Morning Herald*, and me, an Australian journalist living in Bhutan.

This is the first time Bhutan has invited the international press to cover an event, and government officials are both welcoming and wary. Bhutan, which for centuries was closed to outsiders, has opened its borders a little, but is still highly suspicious of Western ways. The foreign media have been issued with national costumes to ensure that we do not lower the tone of the day. All of us were up before dawn to be helped into these formal garments, which the Bhutanese happily wear every day. Women journalists and photographers are covered neck to toe in colourful *kiras*, made of densely woven cloth wrapped tightly around the body. The men are in *ghos*, which resemble wildly striped dressing-gowns: these are worn belted at the waist, leaving a billowing pocket at the front. We have been herded into a secluded area, out of everyone's way, and been told to stay here.

Barefoot dancers with curtains of yak hair covering their faces enter the courtyard and leap around in the frosty morning like mad, drunken sprites. Monks follow, carrying colourful parasols. A farmer parades a snowy-white sheep with an extra horn coming out of its nose, which looks macabre but is considered very auspicious, and therefore a gift befitting a King on this grandest of days. The air is filled with the hypnotic chanting of hundreds of monks, a deep rumbling that we can feel in our bones. When they stop, there is a vacuum of sound that leaves our ears ringing.

As the sun sets on Coronation Day and the new King finally goes home to his palace, the pace is quickening in the offices of *Bhutan Observer.*

There is an eight-page pictorial wraparound to finish, multiple stories about the day's festivities to lay out and, when the editors aren't looking, Facebook pages to update with personal comments about this momentous occasion. The kitchen staff bring another round of sweet tea, *momos* and raw, whole chillies, to keep everyone going. The atmosphere is industrious but also elated. It is the controlled panic of a newsroom as it approaches deadline on a big news day.

Overwhelmed with the high emotion of it all, the features editor pokes his head out of the window and whoops loudly into the night. A few minutes later four unsmiling policemen appear in the office and chastise him for unruly behaviour. What if a foreign dignitary saw you, they ask. He tries to argue but gives up, hanging his head in shame until they're gone.

After the three days of celebrations the rest of the international press will leave, but I'm lucky enough to stay. I'm two months into a 12-month posting as media consultant to *Bhutan Observer,* a new weekly, bilingual newspaper. This is a pivotal moment in the country's history: the kingdom is famously secretive, and inviting the world press to report on the coronation is but one indication that there has been a fundamental change in the way they do things. As Bhutan offers the outside world a glimpse into its traditions, it is also opening itself up to scrutiny within the country, through a growing independent media.

The country is suddenly awash with fresh-faced, untrained young reporters, poking their noses into other people's business, asking inappropriate questions of their elders and exposing some of the society's underbelly. Many don't like it. Others are in shock or denial as the newspapers reveal staggering figures for domestic violence, high-level corruption and rampant alcoholism, which are so obviously at odds with the country's Buddhist values. It is not how the Bhutanese see themselves or want the outside world to see them. Some are unsure if the press should be allowed to write about such unpleasant topics – how can reporters ask such rude questions of their superiors? It's just not Bhutanese, they say. The move to democracy and modern media is requiring many adjustments.

Nevertheless, this country of mystical, tantric rites, where the King is a deity and yogis still retreat to caves, is embracing the information age on its own terms – often with an ethical rigour and sophistication that we in industrialised countries could learn from. Newspapers, the internet and mobile phones are opening up a vast new public space where, for the first time, Bhutanese citizens are discussing things that matter to them. This little Himalayan kingdom faces many of the same challenges as we do, but their responses come from a different philosophical and cultural wellspring. The country is only just emerging from the feudal system, and joining the modern world in an intellectually and spiritually robust way. It is compelling to watch.

1

A Truly Bhutanese Newspaper

Bhutan Observer is owned by Tenzin Wangdi, 47, and his wife, Phuntsho Wangmo, 38. Tenzin is the head of the company while Phuntsho, who looks after the day-to-day running of the newspaper, is very much its heart.

I first came to know this remarkable family in 2002 when my partner, Mal Watson, was producing the film *Travellers & Magicians*, written and directed by Dzongsar Jamyang Khyentse Rinpoche, a highly revered Bhutanese lama who travels the world teaching on Buddhism and also makes movies. Phuntsho worked as production secretary and, while Mal came and went from remote locations during shooting, our baby daughter Kathryn and I lived with her family on the outskirts of Thimphu. She has four adult sisters and one of them is married to her husband's brother. Kathryn and I spent four months in their large interconnected household, treated partly as honoured guests, partly as honorary cousins.

One night in 2002, while drinking too much Bhutanese whisky with Phuntsho and Tenzin, we talked late into the night about what it might be like to run a newspaper in Bhutan. The country had only one newspaper, the government-owned *Kuensel*, which had been around for more than 30 years. Tenzin and his older brother were already in the printing business, publishing prayer books for monasteries and school texts. They saw newspapers as a natural extension of that business.

It was just idle, fanciful talk until early in 2006, when the Fourth King unexpectedly invited the public to submit proposals to launch private newspapers. His vision for Bhutan to become a democracy required a vibrant, independent media that would hold the government to account. The family had a month to put together a proposal. To their great surprise, they were successful. Mal and I had returned to Sydney when Phuntsho emailed us to announce she had given birth to a baby boy *and* a newspaper.

The Fourth King had granted two licences for weekly newspapers to be printed in English as well as in the national language, Dzongkha, and distributed nationally. A consortium of 24 wealthy businesspeople was licensed to publish *Bhutan Times*, and Phuntsho's family was licensed to publish *Bhutan Observer.*

The family is neither poor nor rich, but somewhere comfortably in between, owning the printing business as well as a hardware shop. Like most middle-class Bhutanese, they have maids and employ a full-time weaver in their home, but they don't go on buying trips to Thailand to furnish their homes or buy CD players and modern appliances like the very wealthy. They live modestly, hanging their clothes on nails in the walls and spending their holidays visiting their village, three days' travel to the east.

Before starting *Bhutan Observer,* they had no experience of media beyond publishing prayer books, watching BBS and occasionally reading *Kuensel.* They had little interest in politics and no friends in government. Yet suddenly they found themselves about to launch a newspaper.

The country's only trained journalists already worked at *Kuensel,* so the family looked around for capable people in their social circles.

One stood out: Dr Sonam Kinga, who at 33 could speak eight languages, had authored several highly respected books and translated Sophocles' play *Antigone* into Dzongkha. For a brief moment he was also one of Bhutan's most recognisable faces, acting as the monk in *Travellers & Magicians.*

What he lacked in media experience he more than made up for in intelligence, education and a sophisticated worldview, which he developed while studying in Japan and Canada. The family appealed to his desire to help Bhutan through the growing pains of democracy, and he agreed to come on board – but only for a year. Ultimately he wanted a bigger role in the new democracy: he intended to stand for election to the country's National Council.

The family made Dr Kinga founding editor-in-chief. His first task was to train staff in a job he didn't know. He interviewed arts graduates of the new Royal University of Bhutan and asked them to write an essay on the role of media in a democracy. Those best able to write in English were invited for interviews.

Senior journalist Tandin Pem, 23, remembers her interview. Dr Kinga asked what stories she would cover in a village. Tandin replied, 'I will report on sale of maize, *tengma* [corn flakes] and other items.' She got the job. The rest of the staff were mostly relatives and looked after distribution, advertising and layout, figuring out how to do their jobs as they went along. The family invited monks to the office to perform *pujas* – a Buddhist blessing of chanting, waving incense and blowing trumpets – to dispel obstacles and ensure a harmonious beginning.

The first editions of *Bhutan Observer* were cobbled together in June 2006 behind Thimphu's main street in a ramshackle wooden hut with gaps in the floorboards, which sat atop a sea of mud. Dzongsar Khyentse Rinpoche wrote a feature for the launch issue about whether Buddhists could kill cockroaches. (The short answer is no.) There were also photos of Her Royal Highness Princess Ashi Sonam Dechan Wangchuck launching the newspaper, and a variety of businesses paid for space to wish the newspaper well.

The rest of the newspaper was devoted to the country's elections, featuring photos of farmers and villagers sitting under trees as they discussed what democracy might mean. Other articles explained how to vote and who the different candidates were, and gave news on the Fourth King. The weekly paper had 14 pages and an initial ambitious print run of 15,000 across the two editions. It cost 10 ngultrum (Nu.10), or about A$0.27.

After the first newspapers started hitting the streets of Thimphu and reaching the remote villages, the family set about determining a specific vision for the newspaper. There was more to this than just a printing business; they had a social responsibility. How could they do that justice? What did it mean? They knew what they didn't want – celebrity scandals, page-three girls, and Hollywood or Bollywood starlets. That would not benefit their society. So how could a newspaper perform within the context of the nation's prevailing Buddhist principles? How could they reflect and reinforce the best of Bhutan? How could they provide a counterpoint to outside culture coming in through Indian television?

Phuntsho and Tenzin invited some of Bhutan's most respected intellectuals, from senior monks to teachers, to be part of a conclave to help them work it out. None were businesspeople: Phuntsho and Tenzin weren't thinking in terms of profit. Rather, the family wanted their newspaper to benefit the community, so they chose people who were well known for their integrity and wisdom.

After a day of lively discussion they ended up with a thoroughly Bhutanese mission statement for their newspaper.

Bhutan Observer guiding principles

> That all things exist in interdependence is an age-old wisdom, and we at *Bhutan Observer* truly believe in this. We recognise that we are an integral part of this society and have a role to play in reporting the news in a fair and balanced way. Our sole objective is to uphold and strengthen the values and principles that bind this small but great kingdom together. We are a voice with a conscience, and our efforts are aimed at enriching people's lives through unbiased content intended to inform, educate and entertain.
>
> The world is in constant flux, often changing at a confusing pace, and only through recognising our relationship with our surroundings and by active participation in events that shape our lives can we create conditions for a positive future. As a media agency, it is our honour to provide opportunity for such reflection and interaction.

From the start, Phuntsho wanted 'a truly Bhutanese newspaper' – Bhutanese voices telling Bhutanese stories, not material downloaded from the internet. She felt there was enough coverage of international news and celebrities on cable television. She wanted stories about daily life in Bhutan. She built up a team of reporters in Thimphu, and four rural correspondents provided a stream of fascinating features from the villages: the town where men believe their wives have crooked vaginas; the ghost that lives in a rock; and the elderly couple doing a three-year pilgrimage around the country, falling to their knees at each step to lay their forehead on the ground.

The decorative icons of each section, or dinkuses as they are known in newspaper rooms, are distinctly Bhutanese. The opinion page is represented by a lit butter lamp to symbolise the illumination brought to difficult issues; the features page uses a face removing a mask to symbolise showing us ourselves; and the insights page, the spiritual heart of the paper, has a decorative sword to symbolise cutting through delusion to achieve clarity and wisdom.

Mal and I followed the newspaper launch from our home in Sydney. Mal had finished *Travellers & Magicians* and was marketing it around the world, and I had written *A Baby in a Backpack to Bhutan*, a memoir about the making of the film, and had started teaching various journalism subjects at university. Phuntsho sent us the first editions of *Bhutan Observer*, which Mal and I pored over, before emailing back our comments. For the next 18 months we continued to swap emails about *Bhutan Observer*'s progress and family news. Then Phuntsho had an idea. Would the three of us consider coming to Bhutan for a year? Mal and I could help her and Tenzin navigate this brave new world of media, and I could teach journalism skills to the reporters and editors.

It was an intriguing idea and we were considering it when one afternoon, as we sat in traffic on Parramatta Road, Kathryn, aged six, asked from the back seat:

'Want longer lasting sex?'

She was reading aloud from a lurid red and yellow billboard spruiking a dodgy nasal spray.

'What does *that* mean?' she asked.

Mal and I looked at each other. We could leave behind Sydney's traffic jams and consumer culture, to spend a year with Phuntsho's family working on their new newspaper?

Yes please.

2

Excellent Abundance

Bhutan is a landlocked country of about 47,000 square kilometres – roughly the size of Switzerland. Wedged between China and India, it is like a pebble between two massive boulders. Only eight pilots in the world are qualified to fly into Paro, weaving around the 5,500-metre peaks and skimming above farmhouse roofs to land at what the *Daily Mail* has called the world's most dangerous airport.

Phuntsho picks us up, and we immediately see that Bhutan has moved into the communications age: two mobile phones dangle from lanyards around her neck. Five years ago her family was one of the few households in Thimphu to have a landline phone. It was on an impossibly long, tangled cord, which the family carried up and down the stairs, only for the connection to drop out. Now mobile phones are so commonplace that Phuntsho has one to make calls and one to receive calls, thereby getting the best of both deals offered by two competing phone carriers. As we bounce along the national highway in the company jeep, she keeps in touch with her printers, monitoring the progress of the week's new edition as it rolls off the presses.

Thimphu, Bhutan's capital, sits in a high-altitude valley surrounded by slopes covered in cypress and pine. People live in suburbs scattered along a winding river, the Wang Chhu, lined with willows. I notice satellite dishes on house roofs or half-hidden in garden shrubbery. They are illegal and prolific.

Phuntsho has organised everything. Kathryn will attend school with her ten-year-old daughter, Renee. The Bhutanese government won't give working visas to both halves of a couple, so this time Mal will be the full-time parent. The United Nations Development Program will pay me a subsistence wage for three months, and after that ... well, Phuntsho says she will figure something out. She has rented us a three-bedroom apartment a street away from hers in Lower Motithang, a middle-class suburb full of similar apartment blocks. There is a small grocery shop on the ground floor, and our apartment is up four flights of stairs. She has borrowed enough furnishings from her extended family for us to be comfortable. Kathryn's wardrobe is a grey office filing cabinet, and we sleep under a doona covered in pictures of Second World War tattoos.

Our living room has a wall of windows. It takes us just two days to realise that this is a problem: the apartment block next door is so close – a couple of metres away – that neighbours over three levels can see right in. Once they discover that foreigners have moved in, we become their favourite pastime. They line up at their windows to watch us. Westerners who make it to Bhutan usually come to trek on one of its world-renowned mountains. They might spend a day in Thimphu buying souvenirs in the main street, but they don't move in next door.

At first we smile politely and wave back, hoping our novelty will wear off. It doesn't and we feel like exhibits in a zoo. We learn to live with the curtains closed.

Phuntsho drives us to a shop in the main street to buy Kathryn's uniform for Sunshine School. It is an Aladdin's cave of interconnecting rooms with towering bundles of woven cloth lining every wall. The woman behind the counter asks the name of Kathryn's school and her age, and then pulls out a pale pink silk undershirt, called the *wonju*, which has no buttons or zips but sleeves that reach to her knees. Over the top of this, the woman wraps a green, purple and pink striped *kira*, whipping it back and forth, making folds at the front and back, tucking and poking, then securing it at the shoulders with large pink nappy pins. Kathryn is fascinated.

Another woman brings a long woven belt in pink and green stripes. She tells Kathryn to breathe in as they wrap it round and round her waist, pulling tightly. When I protest they just laugh, telling me it has to be tight, *very* tight. It is the Bhutanese way. Finally they produce a *toego*, the jacket, which is the same vivid green as the stripe in the *kira*. They roll the undershirt's long sleeves back over the jacket cuffs, and, after some more tucking and poking, pin the jacket closed with another nappy pin.

Kathryn looks gorgeous – elegant and exotic, all three feet of her. *This is my school uniform*, she mouths to Mal and me, her eyes large and round. It sure beats the navy skirt and yellow shirt of her Sydney primary school.

On the first school morning, Phuntsho and Renee come over to show us how to re-create this ensemble. I take notes and draw diagrams. Start on the right at the back. First corner on the left shoulder, wrap back and around, pin, drape, fold. Pin at the right shoulder. Tuck. Secure back fold. Wrap the belt tightly. Create a pocket at the chest. The flap should be at the front on the left. If it's on the right, you've blown it. Start again. It is like a Rubik's cube made out of fabric, and I start to dread being left alone in a room with one. Phuntsho promises that she and Renee will come every morning before school until we are confident we can do it on our own.

A few minutes' walk from our new home is Changangkha Lhakhang, a stunning 12th-century temple where mothers bring their children to be blessed. They climb the ancient stone steps, carrying offerings of butter for the lamps. Old women spend daylight hours shuffling around the temple, spinning prayer wheels as they go, sending blessings into the world. Phuntsho brought me here in 2002 when Mal was away filming and Kathryn was an eight-month-old baby who wouldn't sleep. I remember climbing the 108 worn stone steps, passing other women, babies tied to their backs with shawls. Kathryn and I were near demented from lack of sleep but after that visit we both slept like … babies. I have a big soft spot for this *lhakhang.*

Phuntsho brings us here before our first workday to make offerings and light butter lamps. She seeks blessings for Kathryn as she starts at her new school, and makes aspirations that together she and I may bring compassion and wisdom to the newspaper office.

Bhutan Observer takes up the top two floors of a new building at the end of Thimphu's main street, Norzin Lam. There are about 50 people on staff. Founding editor-in-chief Dr Sonam Kinga has moved on to government as he had hoped. The newspaper has had two editors-in-chief in the two years since, and is currently run by Needrup Zangpo, a former researcher in the Ministry of Education. He has little media experience, but he is passionate about the newspaper and is learning the job by doing it.

The reporters, men and women in their early twenties, work at computers in partitioned work stations, while the section editors (news, features and arts), all men in their thirties, have small glass-walled offices. There is a little balcony, out of view of the editors, where two-thirds of the staff sneak off for a cigarette. Bhutan made world headlines when it became the world's first non-smoking nation in December 2004, with the sale of tobacco declared to be illegal. Three months later it banned smoking in public spaces. The fine is Nu.10,900, or A$300, the equivalent of two months' salary for the average civil servant. The ban hasn't stopped smoking, just increased its rebellious appeal; cigarettes are bought in India and sold on the black market. Smoking is popular among the reporters and advertising staff.

I work closely with Phuntsho, writing business proposals and discussing all the challenges faced by a fledgling media mogul in this new democracy. I imagine some are the headaches of media proprietors everywhere. Others are uniquely hers.

Editorial isn't meeting the Thursday-night deadline. Two government departments haven't paid their advertising bills this month, so it will be a struggle to pay staff. She doesn't have enough cars to deliver the newspapers around Thimphu. Distribution to other parts of the country is taking days, so our news is old by the time it arrives, whereas *Kuensel* owns a printing press in the east, so their news is always fresh. The Dzongkha edition is expensive to produce and attracts no advertising, but the licence requires the company to continue to publish it.

Phuntsho is full of ideas to make the newspaper better, but she doesn't have enough staff. She needs reporters, editors for the different sections, and IT personnel for a new webpage. There are rumours of new newspapers coming, which will compete for the already limited numbers of readers, advertisers and staff.

The name Phuntsho Wangmo means 'powerful mother of excellent abundance', and it suits her. She and her husband share a grand vision for the newspaper. While Tenzin previously ran the printing presses of his family's publishing company, her own background is in hotel management. She worked for a year at a famous 15th-century hotel in Austria, known for accommodating Mozart, before returning to Bhutan to run the family's hardware shop. While she has no experience in media, she recognises its power and possibilities. She is also one of those people who are successful in whatever they choose to do. It's a combination of ideas, energy and a terrier-like quality – she just doesn't give up.

She starts her day before dawn in the shrine room of her apartment, saying prayers and making offerings, as a way to counteract the human habit of selfishness and instead to practise giving. Every morning she reaffirms her commitment to benefit all sentient beings and it's in that frame of mind that she arrives at the office. I marvel at it every day.

Phuntsho puts me in an office next door to hers, and most mornings she calls me in to discuss a new idea that has occurred to her overnight. Anything could have triggered it – a story on BBS news the previous evening, a chance remark from another parent as she drops her daughter at school, or something that's happening in her extended family.

One morning she is worried about education. How can we improve the children's pages? What do children need? How can we get them involved, encourage them? Before her handbag hits her desk we are planning new puzzles and listing possible sponsors to provide free copies to schools.

Another morning she is unhappy that young people moving to Thimphu are losing respect for the traditional life of the farmer. 'How can the newspaper reawaken respect for our farmers?' she asks. 'They are the *real* Bhutanese.'

After a visit to Thimphu's glamorous new five-star, Indian-owned Taj Tashi hotel, she is concerned that Buddhist symbols are being used as decorations. The reception desk is adorned with a painting of Buddha's head, door handles are designed to resemble ceremonial trumpets, and a fountain is in the shape of a huge butter lamp. The experience crystallises something that has been annoying her for weeks. She points out that a Thimphu meat shop has taken the name OM, the sacred Sanskrit word. Bhutanese airline stewardesses are wearing half-*kiras* with modern *toegos*. Phuntsho thinks they look more Thai than Bhutanese.

'We must stop this cultural dilution. It is not good for Bhutan,' she says. We plan a lift-out about Bhutanese culture, inviting spiritual leaders and government ministers to contribute.

When I'm not with Phuntsho I run weekly writing workshops, attend news conferences and edit stories for the newspaper. On deadline night, Thursday, I sit with the editors, suggesting headings and captions and helping to lay out pages.

I have to constantly adjust my understanding of news principles to fit with the Bhutanese view of the world. Sometimes I find myself in a parallel universe, trying to rationally discuss the news value of something completely non-rational.

One Thursday evening we discuss a caption for a photo of a baby born with four arms. I see the child and feel sad, thinking in terms of deformity and disability. But I realise with surprise that the arts editor is thinking in terms of the divine: he sees the baby as a form of the Buddhist deity Mahakala, who is often depicted with four arms. Mahakala represents ultimate reality and is highly revered, so having Mahakala in your family is a gift. The news value in the story is to celebrate the child's sacredness.

The discussion reminds Needrup of a *Kuensel* story a few years earlier. A boy from the country's east was recognised as the reincarnation of his family's bull, which had died ten years earlier. As a toddler he used to climb down the stairs to where the animals slept. His parents would find him in the morning curled up asleep in the bull's old pen. He had a very thick neck and even in Grade 5 preferred to walk on all fours. The boy would be about 14 now, and together we discuss what he might be like. Does he still behave like a bull? Needrup thinks it is time for a follow-up. A perfect story for *Bhutan Observer*'s feature pages.

Phuntsho has been planning a special magazine to celebrate 100 years of the Wangchuck dynasty to coincide with the coronation in two months, and she asks me to take over as editor. This is the company's first attempt at producing a glossy magazine for sale, and if it works, they might do more. One of my first tasks is to write some advertisements for potential advertisers. Phuntsho says people would like to buy space to praise the outgoing King and welcome the new King.

This is how Bhutanese businesses advertise – they don't say *come to our petrol station* or *visit our shop*; they say *we love our King*. With absolutely no idea what I'm doing, I have a go at writing some copy: 'Congratulations to our glorious new King. May his reign be long and harmonious.'

I show it to Phuntsho. I can tell by her wan smile that it isn't what she wanted. I haven't fully appreciated the attitude to the King. I have to write more, much more. I have another go:

> Humble felicitations to the wise and compassionate leadership of our ruling dynasty for all the glories of the past 100 years and welcome His Majesty Jigme Khesar Namgyel Wangchuck to the Dragon Throne. On the auspicious occasion of his coronation we, his loyal subjects, offer our unwavering dedication and devotion. Long may he reign. All glory to our beloved Druk Gyalpo.

Phuntsho grins when I show it to her. She says I'm *beginning* to get the hang of it. I come up with 100 variations, each more flowery than the last. My tributes are bought by businesses and families, even regions, wanting to publicly honour their new King. They pay for a quarter of a page, a half-page or a full page.

Stories for the magazine start to arrive from all directions, written by editors on the newspaper and freelance writers. A couple of them are interesting personal stories about meeting the Kings; others cover aspects of Bhutanese culture. In a management meeting we settle on a name for the magazine – *Faces of Bhutan* – accompanied by the tagline 'Extraordinary stories of everyday people'.

Then we strike a major problem. Great stories, but the newspaper has no photos. It is a dreadful irony that tourists pour into the country with their Nikons and Leicas, taking beautiful photos that fill their albums at home, yet there are few photos in Bhutan available to us. There are no photo agencies or professional Bhutanese photographers.

The newspaper's photographer is self-taught, and his temperamental staff camera has only photos of MPs to go with newspaper stories. Tenzin says they will buy a decent SLR camera in Delhi and get someone to bring it across, but that will take time.

So I look on the internet. *Vogue Australia* recently ran a fashion shoot set in Bhutan. Japanese photographer Kenro Izu is having an exhibition in New York of photos taken in Bhutan. Flickr is full of photos taken by tourists with good cameras. I email them all, requesting permission to publish their photos in a new magazine but explaining we have no budget to pay for them. I am astounded at the goodwill and selflessness that comes winging back to me. Kenro Izu, who is recognised as one of the world's best photographers, uploads for us his whole exhibition about to go on display in the Rubin Museum of Art – a series of breathtaking black-and-white portraits of the Fifth King, monks and reincarnate lamas. The *Vogue* photographers are just as helpful, sending photos of Bhutanese life: a mass of monks draped across whitewashed monastery steps, a gaudily decorated truck, leering animal masks on display in a shop. Such generosity is not normal behaviour in the publishing world. There is something about this little country, nestled in the clouds, that creates fond feelings in everyone who visits. Normal rules of copyright and financial compensation need not apply. I love it.

Still, we need more photos of the Kings. The features editor phones the palace to explain our problem, and two days later the secretary to the Fifth King arrives with the latest MacBook under his arm. He shows us slide after slide of intimate family moments: the Kings informally holding hands, sitting on matching thrones or inside private rooms at the palace; the Fifth King playing archery, posing with his dogs, wearing a bear fur hat and cuddling a little girl with a bamboo tepee on her head. They are all fantastic – the Fifth King is genetically blessed and seems unable to take a bad photo. But to my journalist's eye, what is even better is that they are all new. Most shops and homes have the approved royal portraits on their walls, the same half-a-dozen or so formal poses. But these photos show the King and royal family as never seen before.

The editors make a selection of 44 photos and it takes all my willpower to shut up and leave the decision to them. I know my place: as a foreigner, it would be inappropriate for me to join in this discussion about their King.

Phuntsho hires Tashi, a graphic designer who works for the civil service by day and comes in late at night after I've gone home. I leave him piles of notes on a printout, and when I come in each morning there is a new page in my computer, beautifully laid out, ready to be edited.

I try to understand the Bhutanese aesthetic, and Tashi and I produce four possible covers. I lay them out on Tenzin's coffee table for the editors and management to choose. They all pounce on the same one, which shows the Fifth King cuddling a little girl. They explain that she is from the remote Layap tribe, one of the poorest in the country. When I see the image through their eyes, it is indeed the winning shot. The affection between the child and the King says it all.

The finished *Faces of Bhutan* magazine is sent on a disc to Delhi to be printed on bright, white paper imported from Finland and trucked back to Thimphu. It is advertised in *Bhutan Observer* and sold in three Thimphu bookshops, as well as at the airport and a few tourist shops. It instantly creates a buzz.

Druk Air wants hundreds of copies for their planes. Druk Seed Corporation phones to request 20 copies. Two Japanese tourists wander up the three flights of stairs of the *Bhutan Observer* building and into Phuntsho's office, looking to buy copies of this magazine they keep hearing about. Government departments chase the advertising staff for copies. The office maid, who can't speak English or read, asks for a magazine because she heard the sweeper had one. Phuntsho is delighted and tells her she is an important part of *Bhutan Observer* so of course she should have one.

But we really know it is a success when the Fourth King's secretary rings and says His Majesty would like a copy. He had been visiting his third Queen when he saw a copy lying on her table and thought it looked 'interesting'.

'We've never sent anything to the King before,' says Phuntsho, who drops everything and personally drives up the winding road above Thimphu to deliver a magazine to the palace gates. She doesn't stop smiling for a week.

3

Braying Donkeys

Everywhere we go, people stare. Mal has been coming to Bhutan for 15 years and is used to it, and in the office I ceased to be exotic by the end of the first week. But Kathryn, as the only child with red hair and blue eyes at her school, is finding it harder to blend in. The other children tease her about the smell of her Vegemite sandwiches. A couple of kindy kids follow her into the toilet – all open cubicles – to see if she is the same under her *kira* as them, until Renee follows and shoos them out.

People in the street reach out to touch Kathryn's face, smiling and speaking to her kindly, but she hates it. She asks me not to sing in the car with the window down in case it draws further attention to us, and I am not allowed to pick her up from school unless I wear a *kira* and a black wig.

Mal does his best to help. He puts the Vegemite away and asks her to describe what everyone else is eating. Chilli. Curry. Meat. Rice. He buys a flat skillet pan from the market and gets up early to make Indian-style chapattis for her lunch. He has never made them before, but having lived in India for 12 years and eaten his fair share, he thinks he can figure it out. He tries a little curry. Kathryn says it's better than Vegemite sandwiches, but brings home her lunches untouched. Finally, they settle on fried rice. Mal buys a tiffin box and a plastic hand basket for her to carry it in, just like the other children do. And at the end of the school day he waits discreetly near the school gate, ready with a welcoming smile, but not *too* close or *too* visible.

He helps with her homework and soon they can both draw the Bhutanese flag (orange and yellow with a black and white dragon), and name the national flower (blue poppy) and animal (takin). Kathryn learns to draw the four tools of a farmer – axe, hammer, shovel and bucket – and that pushing and shouting are 'bad habits', while helping and being quiet are 'good habits'.

At the office Phuntsho works hard to get me to wear a *kira* and I give it my best shot, really I do. Kathryn, by now skilled at dressing in her own *kira*, helps me into it. But whenever I wear it, well-meaning Bhutanese feel obliged to help. As I move through the day, people – from reporters to bureaucrats visiting the office to strangers in the street – step forward to adjust me. I feel gauche and realise that no matter what I do, to the Bhutanese I don't look right. I settle on a compromise. Two days a week I struggle into the *kira*, and resign myself to being prodded, while the rest of the week I wear pants with knee-length Indian tunic-style shirts. This isn't nearly as glamorous as the *kira*, but it is comfortable and no-one feels compelled to poke at me.

The men in the office all wear *ghos*, beautifully tailored and vividly coloured, with a crisp white undershirt. The starched white cuffs fold back over the sleeves of the *gho*. Dressing in a *gho* is as complicated as trying to drape a *kira*. It is an oversized robe that must be folded, tucked and belted to create a pocket at the front and two knife-edge pleats at the back. Phuntsho says most wives help their husbands dress each morning. Sometimes I see younger men in the office, those without wives, fixing each other's pleats at the start of the day. It always makes me smile.

In their national dress, the Bhutanese men look impossibly stylish in a way that men in the West never do, except perhaps a Scotsman in a dress kilt. A dinner suit doesn't come close. At *Bhutan Observer*, the staff wear their *ghos* with varying degrees of elegance. Some fuss with their hems, to preserve their modesty as they sit. Others plonk themselves down with gusto – bare knees akimbo above the low table, underpants on clear display.

My news writing classes start slowly. The biggest challenge is getting the reporters and editors to turn up. It's nothing personal. It would seem that few meetings are ever fully attended. Nor are people punctual. No-one else seems surprised by this behaviour, so I try to go along with it, smiling endlessly, which is what everyone else around me seems to be doing. But inside I feel like I'm operating through a fog.

I'm told the Bhutanese are deferential to authority. In her memoir *Beyond the Sky and the Earth: A Journey into Bhutan*, Canadian schoolteacher Jamie Zappa writes that children learn not to question their parents, teachers, Kings, government officials or superiors of any other type. I imagine what I must look like to the reporters. I represent management, I'm the same age as their parents and I'm standing in front of a whiteboard. I'm also a *chillip*, which is slang for 'foreigner'. While no Bhutanese will translate it for me precisely, I suspect it's not entirely complimentary, reflecting their mixed views of foreigners. We seem to represent sophistication and modernity, but also moral decay.

All these factors make for a stilted start. In our first classes I do a lot of talking while they look at me blankly. They don't contribute or engage in discussion, but sit passively, their relief obvious when our time is up and they can file out the door.

Before I left Australia, the then editor-in-chief of *Bhutan Observer* had emailed me the training program he believed the staff needed.

Hard news, soft news, how to write news style, how to write a feature, how to prepare for an interview, how to write a profile, where to find stories, establishing beats, and so on. I've come prepared with notes, handouts and writing exercises I've used when teaching journalism students in Sydney, but with the material adapted for Bhutanese sensibilities. John Smith waving a gun in a Sydney shopping centre becomes Tashi Dorji waving his knife in Thimphu's vegetable market. The journalists and editors practise writing a news lead from these facts. They are polite, but obviously uninterested.

It is only when I ask them to write a lead about a fictitious government minister that I see a spark. A minister? They won't talk to us, says a reporter. Bhutanese government ministers won't answer questions. I ask why not. The change in the room is palpable: the reporters and editors drop their pens in their enthusiasm to join in. The reporters are struggling with access to ministers, as the MPs refuse to talk to them – at all. One reporter tells of how a minister ordered her to leave a public meeting, and how humiliated she felt to be singled out and publicly chastised just for doing her job.

Freedom of the press has been written into the new constitution, and the Fourth King has made it clear that part of the role of the new newspapers is to hold the government accountable. And yet ... the Bhutanese have lived for centuries with a rigid social hierarchy. Even ordinary people share the view that reporters should not question their superiors. Democracy or no democracy, it just is not polite.

Since the 17th century, the Bhutanese have adhered to a code of behaviour called the *driglam namzha*. It was created by Zhabdrung Rinpoche, the founding father of Bhutan. Believed to be the reincarnation of a famous monk, Zhabdrung Rinpoche was made abbot of a Tibetan monastery, but fled to Bhutan in 1616, aged just 22, when the ruler of the region decided to install his own candidate. At that time Bhutan was largely lawless, riven by violent tribal feuds. Zhabdrung Rinpoche sought to unite the country, both politically and culturally.

As the reincarnation of a revered Buddhist master, he had the moral authority to do so. In just three decades he founded a national government; imposed law and order; designed the national dress, including different coloured shawls to denote one's social standing; created a new style of architecture; choreographed lama dances to be performed at new religious festivals called *tshechus*; and established rules of behaviour for civil society. This code of conduct for everyday life evolved out of monastic vows and cover the whole gamut of individual behaviour, from the Buddhist ideal of striving to be aware of one's own state of mind to showing good manners, maintaining social harmony and always respecting superiors.

The arrival of democracy – and the media – means that this social hierarchy is beginning to break down. When journalists wearing humble white shawls ask questions of government ministers in their superior orange shawls, the formality of centuries is turned on its head. The reporters seem to have adapted to the changing dynamic and are asking the right questions of government, but some of the MPs are having trouble with the new arrangement. Just because the country is now a democracy doesn't mean VIPs are happy to be questioned by people they consider socially inferior. Many government ministers are also inexperienced in their roles and don't feel confident under public scrutiny.

I see the government attitude myself. A few weeks after arriving, a senior civil servant from the Ministry of Information and Communications invites me to his office for tea and asks whether I think it is ethical for a journalist to call a minister on Sunday when he is at his child's birthday. It's a loaded question and I'm immediately wary. This is the man who approved my visa. I know how sensitive Bhutan is about foreigners bringing their grubby ways to sully this new media industry. Phuntsho went to great lengths to assure this man and this department that I would be an 'in-house consultant' who would not influence the editorial line of the newspaper. This genteel tea in his office feels like a follow-up interview to check on me now that I'm in the country. I reply that I think it is ethical, though perhaps not polite. He seems satisfied.

The mood of our writing workshops improves as we start to explore the specific needs of the reporters. How can they form relationships with ministers? How can they get the ministers to trust them without compromising their own integrity? We develop ideas for stories that are non-threatening – profiling a different minister each edition about what they have done that week, and so on. The discussions become lively and interesting.

We have a session about finding stories, and talk about what makes news in Bhutan. There are familiar topics, such as accidents on the main highway, forest fires and fuel prices, as well as distinctly Bhutanese issues: the royal family, *tshechus*, yak diseases, potato harvests, stray dogs, elephants trampling maize plantations, and Gross National Happiness.

My favourite part of the week is Monday morning, when *Bhutan Observer* holds its news conference to plan the next issue. The conferences are held in the grand, wood-lined boardroom on the top floor, signalling their importance in the scheme of things. As editor-in-chief, Needrup leads the meetings, which are also attended by the three section editors, six reporters, the political cartoonist, a photographer and me. We sit at tables set up in a big U, watched over by dignified photographs of all five Kings. The kitchen staff bring trays of sweet tea, then withdraw. On auspicious days, the sound of trumpets and horns wafts in from nearby homes or building sites where monks are conducting *pujas*.

In this forum the reporters and editors are outspoken and informed. They gossip, argue and thrash around story ideas, giving me a front-row seat to everything that's happening in the kingdom. Watching them, I feel extraordinarily privileged to be seeing their country through their eyes. Needrup says that working on the newspaper makes you see Bhutan as it is, not how you might like it to be, and at the news conferences I start to glimpse the complexity of this country. Corruption, domestic violence and the economy are discussed alongside miracles and the supernatural.

One day the discussion moves from the government voting to give itself a pay hike, and what that will mean for civil servants and poor villagers, to the *rolong* – tall zombies who 'come at night from the dead place to perform mischief'. A reporter tells of new *rolong* activity in a particular village where she has relatives. She explains to me that many rural homes have small doors to stop the *rolong* entering their homes. '*Rolong* can't bend at the knees,' she whispers.

A reporter suggests a story for the features pages on men in Thimphu wearing makeup. Her younger brother and his friends are copying the Korean rock stars they see on cable television. 'They're called "metrosexuals",' she announces. Needrup is bewildered. *Men wearing makeup? Why would they do that?*

He writes the stories on the whiteboard. Government pay hike, civil servants' pay rates, effect on village poverty, men and makeup, and *rolongs*. The traditional face of Bhutan and the modern: it's the sort of balance he strives for in each edition. He needs all the stories by Thursday to make this week's edition, which goes on sale on Friday.

Although just 31, Needrup has the demeanour of a stern grandfather. When the reporters talk about the new nightclubs springing up around Thimphu, he looks baffled. He works long hours and goes home to his wife and young children. He talks about burying his head under the blankets to drown out his five-year-old daughter's Hindi or Western music. 'Why can't she listen to nice Dzongkha music?' he asks. When he tries to get her to listen to the traditional music of Jigme Drukpa, a Bhutanese hero, she clutches her belly and moans. He shakes his head with dismay.

When people describe Needrup, they often use the word 'solid'. He is tall and square-jawed, with the high cheekbones typical of the country's east, where he was born. He speaks slowly, considering each word, which adds to his sense of gravitas.

Having thrown in a secure career in the civil service to pursue his real passion, journalism, he undertook a one-month course in India and then joined *Bhutan Observer* as deputy editor. When the editor-in-chief, who was known to like his whisky, didn't appear for weeks, Needrup became acting editor-in-chief. It was a meteoric rise after just three months. The three section editors have more experience but lack the commitment, and none of them seem to resent him being catapulted over their heads. Ambition and competitiveness are not valued in this culture. In fact, such traits can be signs of being possessed by a scary spirit, the *gson'dre*. No-one wants that.

Needrup shares the sensibilities of Phuntsho and Tenzin, and wants to produce a quality newspaper that is socially responsible. He is highly principled: I've watched him stand firm against important people who have found their way to his door, seeking favours or requesting that unflattering stories be pulled.

One morning Needrup hears from his family in their village that there is an outbreak of foot-and-mouth disease among farms in the east. Cows are dying, and their butter and milk, contaminated with the virus, cannot be sold. He assigns a reporter to investigate the story. A discussion ensues about different ways of dealing with foot-and-mouth, and Needrup recalls an outbreak from when he was a child.

'We had 28 cows. My father killed two pigs, mixed the pork with maize flour and fed the *whole* pig carcass to the cows. They were cured. The trick is to give them the whole pig.'

I'm reminded that the people in this room are just one step from the land. When they talk about home, they're not referring to their Thimphu residences but the small remote villages where their parents and grandparents live. Here, they are in the bustling capital, part of this exciting, dynamic world of media, government and change. The difference between their lives and their parents' in such a short time is startling.

Needrup gives a lot of thought each week to his editorial column. It appears on page two, above the political cartoon. Both are fearless. I often don't get the joke of the cartoon, but once it's explained to me I'm always impressed. The cartoonist, Chimi Namgyal, is a mild-mannered, talented young man who skewers the government nearly every week.

People in power take notice of page two. Ministers complain that Needrup, like the rest of the media, is always negative. *Why do they have to focus on our shortcomings instead of our successes?* they complain, echoing government ministers all over the world.

One week, after another minister bars a reporter from a public meeting, Needrup locks himself in his office for a couple of hours to write his editorial. He goes in frowning but comes out smiling.

The braying donkeys and barn managers

This is the story of undernourished donkeys plodding under a heavy burden. They feed on a carefully rationed measly diet. The diet comes from a huge barn known among the donkey fraternity as barno because the donkeys are barred from or have no access to it. The system of managing the barno is known as barnocracy and the people who man the system are called barnocrats. The barno contains all kinds of grains. While some are to be consumed only by barnocrats, others are preserved indefinitely for future consumption. Other grains are considered too good to be donkey food. Yet, the donkeys plod on.

The donkeys are responsible for sounding the alarm at any possible sign of mishap or danger in the barnocracy and beyond.

> So they instinctively bray. But the harsh braying displeases many. Horses want the donkeys to neigh in their cadence while birds want them to sing to their tune. Barnocrats want the donkeys to eulogise the rich façade and unknown content of the barno, not bray out the truth of its dark underbelly ... Barnocrats must understand how the donkeys plod. They should realise that, if the donkeys bray, it is in their nature and duty to bray. The donkeys wish that the barnocracy would recognise some fundamental principles of democracy.

The editorial is also posted on the *Bhutan Observer* website. A reader comments that it is marvellous and dubs Needrup the 'George Orwell of Bhutan'.

4

Night-hunting

The colour photograph on the *Bhutan Times* front page should be appealing. A tiny, perfectly formed baby is curled as if asleep, his little fingers just touching his mouth. He has big ears, a snub nose and patches of dark hair.

But looking at the image is like being slapped in the face. It gives you a jarring shock. The baby is dead, a seven-month-old bloody foetus wrapped in a plastic bag and found in a ditch. The accompanying story tells of a 14-year-old Indian maid who hadn't known she was pregnant and reacted to the birth with shock, throwing her baby from a third-storey window.

I know attitudes to death differ in the East and the West. Buddhist practitioners can spend many healthy years preparing for the moment of their death. Funeral ceremonies go on for 49 days. And in a developing country, death happens earlier and often with little privacy or dignity. Back home we are more circumspect, even squeamish, about death; we rarely publish photographs of dead bodies, much less bloody babies.

I feel nauseated and dispirited as I join that day's morning news conference, and I'm not alone. The editors and reporters of *Bhutan*

Observer are outraged by the *Bhutan Times* front page. It is sensationalist, says one. Typical of that newspaper, adds another. People don't want to see that, says Needrup.

The revulsion of the staff is echoed throughout the week in offices, shops and private homes. It becomes the talk of Thimphu. I see a prominent businessman turn the newspaper over in disgust. Another tells me he hid the newspaper from his wife at breakfast, not wanting to upset her.

The youth and inexperience of the editors at *Bhutan Times* is painfully public. They thought the graphic photo would reinforce to readers the tragedy of the baby's death. They had good intentions, but they misjudged public sensitivities.

And they are made to pay for it.

Bhutan InfoComm and Media Authority (BICMA), which regulates the media, notes the groundswell of outrage. It fines *Bhutan Times* Nu.18,000 (about A$495) and sends a tough letter demanding editorial justification for publishing the picture, warning that repeated offences could lead to the cancellation of their newspaper licence. Eleven days after the photo appears, in an act of public contrition, *Bhutan Times* publishes a mea culpa, as well as a letter from one of its readers that seems to reflect the mood of Thimphu.

> Sir,
>
> The picture of the poor unfortunate baby your paper printed sent a chill through my system and left an indelible image of horror not just in my heart but also in my seven-year-old daughter's. It was an extremely crass and insensitive action that disrespected the baby and mother. What purpose did it serve? Such actions might be common elsewhere but not in Bhutan, where we pride ourselves on being a compassionate people of a Buddhist country.
>
> Is it just a matter of time before we have photographers greedily taking pictures of corpses just in case it might come in handy for

> the related article? Are we to expect more such grotesque graphic portrayals as an expression of journalistic freedom? I urge you to practise journalism along the path guided by a moral compass and ethics. Journalism with a heart, please!
>
> Sonam Choden, Motithang

I mention the photo to Kay Kirby Dorji, one of a handful of foreign women who married Bhutanese men and have brought up families in Thimphu. She was a journalist for 25 years on the *Los Angeles Times*, *San Francisco Chronicle* and *Seattle Times*, and first came to Bhutan on a trek in 1986. She ended up marrying the trek leader and is now a full-time resident. Kay is excited about the nascent newspaper industry, though it often makes her shake her head in dismay.

'I would say that *Bhutan Times*, while I love that they try to shake things up, usually they make my blood pressure rise … [by doing] so many things that I would consider to be issues of journalistic ethics, inappropriate or sloppy reporting,' she says.

'First of all, we do have a dearth of journalists and the ones we do have tend to be men. It is a very testosterone-driven news coverage and they are young men, not men who are necessarily mature yet.' She adds, 'I realise they are learning, but at the same time, just being an adult human being, much less a journalist, you should know better.'

Bhutan Times stirs things up again a few weeks later with a front page calling for the Bhutanese tradition of 'night-hunting' to be included in the *Rape Act of 1996*. Under the heading 'Watch out night-hunters' it writes: 'Night-hunting, the practice of men secretly visiting houses of women at night for sex, may become a legal offence, if a recommendation by the National Commission of Women and Children becomes law.'

I read the story over breakfast. It's not the first time I've heard of night-hunting, but it is the first time I've seen it linked to rape. By the time our news conference comes around at 11 am, all the reporters and editors have read the story, and they are not happy.

'Typical of city people to misunderstand this innocent rural pastime,' declares Needrup.

In his family village near Mongar, four days' travel to the east, night-hunting is the way young people choose a romantic partner. It's tradition, he says. It has been done that way for centuries. In Needrup's view, village girl meets village boy, perhaps during the celebrations of a *tshechu* or while helping to harvest neighbours' crops. They like each other and arrange a midnight visit. Needrup recalls walking for two hours on one occasion to call on a girl, only to find his best friend's shoes outside her window. On another occasion he found a friend stuck halfway up a wall.

For *Bhutan Times* to criticise this rural tradition and portray it as rape is, in his mind, unconscionable.

The reporters on *Bhutan Observer* agree with him, vehemently. Again, one of them says it's typical of *Bhutan Times* to be sensationalist. Another tells me that if it wasn't for night-hunting, she and her brothers wouldn't be here – it is how her parents met after noticing each other across the fields while they worked. There was no opportunity for 'dating', so the young man asked if he could visit, the young woman agreed, and that was how they conducted their courtship.

A third reporter explains to me that growing up in a rural area affords little opportunity for privacy. There's no local bar or cinema to visit. Often it is bitterly cold, so even a stroll by the river is out. Chores mean no time off during the day, and without electricity everyone retires together early, ready for another hard day in the fields.

On top of that many poor rural families share one-room huts, sleeping side by side across the floor, perhaps with the parents in one corner behind a curtain. For a young woman to allow a male caller to visit at night would mean the parents would have to know and approve, even while pretending not to know.

I imagine what this must be like in practice. It seems awfully public, your whole family supposedly sleeping nearby. I try not to look shocked but clearly I don't succeed: the reporter laughs at the expression on my face. It's how they do it in remote villages, she says.

On the other hand, a male reporter tells of being chased by a father across the wheat fields when he was discovered climbing in a window. Clearly that father wasn't turning a blind eye to anything.

Later I ask Phuntsho what she thinks of night-hunting. She says that's how her parents started their life together and they went on to have nine children. They are still very happy.

Needrup believes *Bhutan Times* has done rural people a disservice and it is up to *Bhutan Observer* to bring some balance to the discussion. His next editorial, two days later, is a fiery response:

> Things need to be put in perspective once again. We have people, who have little or no rural perspective and experience, indiscriminately painting night-hunting in a negative light. Night-hunting is an integral part of Bhutanese culture in some parts of the country. For generations of young Bhutanese in the eastern villages, it has been their primary means of courtship … it is the rural equivalent of urban dates, discotheques and parties.

The issue of night-hunting touches a chord. Five days later *Kuensel* joins the debate with a dramatic story and picture splashed across their front page under the headline: 'The dark side of night hunting'. Their in-house artist has drawn a man climbing a ladder, his grey *gho* hitched to reveal lurid orange undershorts.

Kuensel's version of night-hunting is terrifying. It recounts the story of a 27-year-old schoolteacher posted to a remote school who was being terrorised by local men at night rattling her front door and trying to climb in her window. The article tells of other young women being accosted by strangers while they slept. 'Girls sound asleep after a day's farm labour had hardly any time to protest before it was too late. The stranger would have crept through the open attic or forced open the poorly shut door or window with a knife to squirm in. The entire business was forced entry they said. Some became pregnant as a result.'

The *Kuensel* story adds fuel to the debate and becomes the talk of the next news conference. Needrup and the reporters are annoyed. Night-hunting is entirely different from *Kuensel*'s depiction. It is consensual. They say Kinley Dorji, the editor-in-chief of *Kuensel* and Bhutan's most celebrated journalist, should know better. From the level of heated discussion, it is obvious that they feel protective of this rural tradition. I start to feel conflicted. Is *Kuensel*'s story accurate and are the *Bhutan Observer* staff in denial? Are rural women being harassed, attacked and demeaned?

Needrup locks himself in his office for a few hours and writes another impassioned defence:

Defining night-hunting

Night-hunting is not related to rape or teenage pregnancy or fatherless children or divorce or drug abuse in any way whatsoever! If a man went to a woman in the night and sexually assaulted her, it is not night-hunting. It is rape. If a gang of men tried to break a window or door of a house in the night, it is not night-hunting. It is vandalism or break-in. If a bunch of men milled about somebody's house in the night shouting, it is not night-hunting. It is hooliganism. If a group of men lingered around a woman's house calling her name in the night, it is not night-hunting. It is verbal harassment. If a man touched or pulled or shoved a woman in a sexually threatening way in the night, it is not night-hunting. It is sexual molestation. If a man slept with a minor in the night, it is not night-hunting. It is child rape. If there are fatherless children or husbandless women, it

> is not night-hunting. It is split-up or divorce. But, if a man visits a woman in the night without committing any of the above crimes, it is none of the above crimes. It is night-hunting, the culture. Period. In the practice of night-hunting, if a man impregnates a woman or a woman conceives, it is not a crime. It is biology.

The discussion continues in the letters pages of all the newspapers. I don't know what the Fourth King's attitude is to night-hunting, but I imagine that, like the rest of Thimphu, he is following the public discussion. The evolving newspaper industry is doing what he intended – presenting a variety of perspectives about a Bhutanese issue, which people are talking about in homes and offices and market stalls across Thimphu.

We are invited to dinner with a Bhutanese couple whom Mal has known for years, and one of the other guests is Kunzang Choden, a feisty woman in her fifties. She was born in Bhutan, educated at a university in India and married a Swiss husband. She is Bhutan's first international novelist and part of *Bhutan Observer*'s advisory board, helping them stay on the ethical straight and narrow.

She brings a different perspective, blaming the divisive debate on the term 'night-hunting'. She says it is not a Bhutanese term translated into English but an English term coined by a Japanese man. It carries connotations that the traditional courtship ritual does not, and she says she cringes every time she hears a Bhutanese person use the term.

'That's not what we called it. It's more like roaming or visiting. It is not top down. We would never have stood for that,' she says emphatically. 'A better translation would be "night-visiting". The tradition was that the boy knocked. The girl could open the door and let him in, or open the door and throw hot ash over him. It was always her choice.'

Kunzang is an opinionated and dynamic woman, and has appeared at writers' festivals all over the world to talk about her novel *The Circle of Karma*, which deals with the restrictive role of her gender. Kunzang is a feminist at heart and in practice. If she sees night-hunting, or night-visiting, as perfectly acceptable then I'm inclined to see it her way.

The debate about night-hunting reveals a fault line within the community and across the different newsrooms. *Bhutan Observer*'s attitude is that *Bhutan Times* and *Kuensel* represent the sophisticated city slickers of Thimphu. They have lost touch with the villages, where the *real* Bhutanese live, and are ignoring the traditional values of the farmer. In the Bhutanese context, to claim you better understand the rural character is to take the moral high ground. The more Bhutanese something is, the better. The less Bhutanese, the more likely it is to be morally suspect.

In this country there are few discernible political shades of left or right, conservative or progressive, or religious differences. No culture wars or history wars. Economic decisions on infrastructure and creating new institutions, such as a High Court, are set out in a series of five-year plans written in consultation with India, which funds the projects.

One place where the newspapers do have a clear ideological difference is in their attitudes to modernisation and rural life. It is why *Bhutan Times* runs a couple of international stories taken from the internet but *Bhutan Observer* does not.

Bhutan Observer is the best newspaper for rural features and daily life in more remote communities. This is both its strength and its weakness. *Bhutan Observer* is seen to be 'more Bhutanese' and therefore more credible, with a moral core. But *Bhutan Times* breaks more stories, which attracts people's attention, and also appeals to younger readers with its stories reprinted from the internet. Phuntsho believes the media has an important role in preserving Bhutanese traditions. This extends to farmers and villages, which she sees as the backbone of Bhutanese cultural life. She does not want democracy and an independent media to diminish their status.

I come to further appreciate the complexities of rural dating during a *Bhutan Observer* weekend workshop. Once the business agenda is covered, the staff break out Bhutanese whisky, served with a dollop of boiling water – just enough to warm it up, but not enough to dilute the alcohol – and Needrup offers to reveal his family secrets for night-hunting, which have been handed down through the generations. He strides the length of the conference table, transforming from grave newsroom boss to Vegas entertainer. The rest of the staff obviously have heard these 'secrets' before and encourage him with ribald comments. One female reporter says she wouldn't have let him in if he had come visiting *her* farm, but another admits she just might have, and everyone hoots with laughter. Needrup starts by paying homage to his two older brothers, who taught him their techniques. He recalls hours spent shivering in bushes while waiting for one or the other.

Needrup's tips for 'night-hunting' young women who don't want to throw ash over you

1. Leave your shoes in the bushes, not at the front door. Everyone in your village knows your shoes and you may have to leave in a hurry so it is stupid to leave them at the door.
2. Don't touch the girl with your bare hands because you will startle her. Coming in from outside, your hands will be very cold. Wrap them in the sleeve of your *gho* or grab a rag and poke her gently with that.
3. Come early and listen outside to the parents talking. As soon as they fall asleep they will go into the 'mother of sleep' and that's the best time to enter the house. If you leave it an hour or

so they will have passed through that 'mother of sleep' and be more likely to wake up.

4. To stop the door from creaking when you open it, urinate on the hinges.
5. To locate the girl in the row of sleeping bodies, use a torch concealed in the palm of your hand. Angle it so that just a few rays poke through your fingers. Once you find her, join her under the blankets as quickly and quietly as possible.
6. Keep your clothes on. You may have to leave in a hurry.
7. Be moderate. Wooden floors can be creaky.
8. Get the girl to wake you before dawn, otherwise the father might make you marry her.

I laugh so hard at the practical nature of his tips that tears roll down my face. I ask about romance and the female reporters on either side of me erupt in giggles. Maybe it's the whisky, or maybe I am hysterically funny; it's hard to tell. The graphic designer, Sushil, comes from the south and says that night-hunting didn't happen in his village. He asks if he can undertake an apprenticeship. Needrup says it would have to be soon, as electricity is killing this wholesome rural practice. When Needrup first started night-hunting, he used matches, which required a particular skill to strike a match, locate the girl quickly and then put out the flame, all without waking anybody else. He demonstrates lighting and extinguishing a match with just one hand, and his dexterity is impressive. Then battery-operated torches arrived, which was good, but now that electricity is spreading further into rural areas, the parents tend to stay up later and if a father is suspicious that an extra body has joined the family row, he just has to flick a switch and you're caught.

Again I get stuck on this image of the whole family being in the same room, lined up like sardines. Phuntsho tells me sometimes the daughters sleep with a parent on either side. Her tone suggests it is the most natural thing in the world. I try to picture my mum and dad, snoring on either side, while a visitor stops by. Surely not. Needrup confirms that such sleeping arrangements are the toughest challenge. The best way around it, he advises, is to pre-arrange for the young lady to nip outside to use the toilet. That method becomes harder in winter, he says, but not impossible.

I wake up in the morning with a throbbing head from the whisky and my jaw aching from laughing. It is undoubtedly the most interesting work conference I've been to.

5

Tashi Pelkhil

At the end of my first three months, the UN funding finishes, but Phuntsho offers to take it over. She has many more big ideas for the newspaper and thinks I can help her realise them. Public discourse is gaining energy after the launch of a fourth newspaper, *Bhutan Today*, in October. It is the country's first daily newspaper, and promises to offer 'The New Perspective'.

After a quick family conference we agree we want to stay, but we can't spend the next nine months in that apartment. It's hard living with our curtains closed and being woken each morning by a family living illegally in our roof, pounding meat with a mallet at 5 am. Neighbours string raw meat on clotheslines on their balconies to dry in the winter sun, which means that as the afternoon wears on, our apartment starts to smell like an abattoir. Some mornings Kathryn wakes coughing as smoke from the *sang* offerings, mostly incense which neighbours burn to start the day, seeps through holes in the walls and into her room. And she is finding school life challenging. It's rowdy and the teachers won't let her take part in the Dzongkha classes, leaving her on her own to colour in for hours at a time.

We glimpse an alternative when we are invited for tea at the home of an expat Dutch woman, whose husband is an engineering geomorphologist for the Ministry of Agriculture.

Cecile and Hans have three children and live at Tashi Pelkhil, a vast estate of about 100 hectares along the Wang Chhu river, just seven minutes from the main street of Thimphu. It is owned by retired army chief General Goenling. Tashi Pelkhil is reached by a discreet little bridge hidden from the road by an ancient wall of *mani* stones, carved with the prayer *Om mani padme hum* as a dedication to the spirits of the area. Locals walk around it as a form of devotion. Over the bridge is a small gatehouse, which is manned at night by three or four soldiers, protecting the General and everyone else on his family estate.

As his four children married and started their own families, the General gave them each a parcel of land. They built a grand two-storey home with high stone walls for themselves, and a more modest house to rent to expat families working for the government or various international aid agencies. The result is an enclave of 13 homes and a bustling multicultural community full of children. There is an Australian woman married to a Bhutanese man, a Danish–Japanese family, plus families from the Netherlands, Uzbekistan and India, as well as the General's own children and their families. The day we visit Tashi Pelkhil, the children are running wild in an Enid Blyton kind of gang, complete with dogs. They have a river, pear and apple orchards, a barn and a corn patch (guarded by a scarecrow) to explore. Sunflowers grow to three metres tall. The private road is perfect for rollerskating. The General, who is more benevolent grandfather than military man these days, has added a fishpond and a horse, especially for the children.

We move into the only vacant home and are quickly absorbed into the Tashi Pelkhil community.

The kids all go to Rosemary's School, a small school of 17 Bhutanese and expat children run by a New Zealand headmistress married to a Bhutanese businessman. We enrol Kathryn, and each morning she skips off to feed the horse before driving to school with Danish dad Jesper.

Most days Mal drives me to work in the little Maruti Alto that we rent from the newspaper, then heads off to the food market. As a 'trailing spouse' he is not allowed to work, officially. But he knows Bhutan well, having come here regularly either to film or to build. As an architect, he has designed homes and retreat centres for Dzongsar Khyentse Rinpoche in India, Canada and Bhutan. While we are here he designs homes for a few Bhutanese friends. He just doesn't charge any money.

The rest of the time he gets around Thimphu. He knows the best stall for lettuce, the grocers who stock butter from Bumthang, and what days the shops are allowed to sell meat, a thorny issue in a Buddhist country. He sometimes bumps into friends he hasn't seen since filming *Travellers & Magicians* here five years ago, and catches up on the gossip.

Like the other families in Tashi Pelkhil, we hire a maid, or, as the expats coyly describe them, a 'helper'. Dolma walks over the bridge every weekday with the helpers of the other families in Tashi Pelkhil village. In the same way the children have formed their own community, the helpers have theirs. They meet most days for lunch or tea at each other's homes, bringing babies and gossip. Courtesy of Dolma, Mal knows pretty much what is going on in every other Tashi Pelkhil home and no doubt they know all our business. When Dolma cooks her signature dish of lasagne, taught to her by her previous Swiss employers, word spreads and neighbours turn up uninvited for dinner.

The helpers also take care of each other. They are part of a Bhutanese underclass, which is illiterate and without citizenship. As non-citizens they are unable to open a bank account. Instead, they operate their own banking collective. Every month they each donate Nu.1,000 (A$27) into a pot, which adds up to Nu.11,000 (A$300). Each month a different woman gets to take home the pot. Dolma says it makes it possible to buy expensive items. Last winter she spent the money on good-quality Korean blankets for her children.

Our family needs are pretty small, and as a result it can be hard for Dolma to find enough to keep herself busy. One day I find my socks neatly filed according to colour. Another day I discover a small tear in my knickers has been hand-stitched. It's a bit disconcerting. She fastidiously washes and rewashes all the plastic bags, pegging them on the clothes line next to Kathryn's toys, which she washes and lines up in a row.

Dolma becomes like a member of our family, bringing her children with her sometimes and inviting her own friends for morning tea in our garden. Phuntsho is gently disapproving, warning that it isn't the way to treat maids. 'Maids stay longer where the bosses are strict,' she says, recounting stories of maids who were lazy or dishonest, or ran off. But like the other expats, we have trouble with such overt social hierarchy. Phuntsho and I return to the topic often, trying to understand our cultural differences. She tells me, sounding both proud and defiant, that her maid eats the same food as the family and always goes out with them. But when I tell her that Mal often drives Dolma and her friend home rather than let them catch the bus at night, she frowns and I know she doesn't approve.

Social hierarchy was one of the ways Zhabdrung Rinpoche established peace among the warring tribes in the 17th century, and it is deeply embedded in the culture. The egalitarian ideals of democracy are making many in Bhutan uncomfortable. Senior journalist Dipika Chhetri writes about it in *Bhutan Today*:

> Before we looked to the West, with all its new-fangled ideas, we had a reasonable, sensible society. Now, we have all kinds of rights

> that are not really rights at all, they are just a breach of somebody else's rights. By what right do we claim the 'right' to be equal? We are not equal. If we were equal we would all be a murky mess of insignificant people. Equality is not something to strive for.

Democracy has arrived in Bhutan without bloodshed, but still the birth is painful. The rapidity of change has left many bewildered. For all the Fourth King's desire to prepare his kingdom for the new era, in a nine-month period the people voted for the first time, finalised their constitution, and saw a change of monarchs.

To many Bhutanese it appears that their way of living – valuing consensus and harmony within their communities – is being suddenly put aside. The Fourth King, who had made the country's decisions and had always been right, wanted the people to take over. They did not want to but, trusting his wisdom in all things, they agreed. Still, it is taking some time to get used to.

In the lead-up to the March 2008 elections, tensions flared all over the country, from remote villages to crowded apartment blocks in Thimphu. People used to bowing to authority were told they were their own authority. They should make up their own minds, have an opinion and, if necessary, disagree. The newspapers carried stories about how the election was splitting communities, villages and even families.

In the midst of all this change, confusion abounds about what democracy means. Before the elections a police officer told *Kuensel*'s Kinley Dorji that a cab driver had objected to being given a speeding ticket, saying, 'Wait until democracy comes in and I have the right to break the rules.'

A senior health bureaucrat declared that the struggling public health system, which cannot cope with the number of patients pouring into the Thimphu hospital each day, should be privatised, because that is democracy, somehow confusing the concept with capitalism.

A distressed farmer asked a government researcher why everyone was suddenly talking about human rights. Did that mean they had been wrong until now?

For the most part, life in Tashi Pelkhil is idyllic, somehow managing to be both cosmopolitan and sleepy. On weekends Kathryn always has somebody to play with, returning home only when it starts to get dark, or she's hungry or covered in mud. The life she leads here perfectly fits our romantic view of what childhood should be like.

One night, however, I'm roused from sleep by the phone ringing beside my head.

'THERE IS A MAN IN MY HOUSE. MAL MUST COME.'

The terror in Cecile's voice brings me instantly awake. I know Hans is away testing soil in a remote forest, a ten-hour drive and then another eight-hour walk away. She is on her own with three young children.

In less than a minute Mal is dressed and sprinting around the corn patch to her house. The night is surreally bright from a near-full moon, which casts long shadows. I lock the door behind him and from our kitchen watch his torchlight bounce around Cecile's property.

Tashi Pelkhil is deserted but thick with the noise of barking dogs. It is like a chain reaction. The neighbours' dogs – Fatty, Thumper and Lucky – have set off the dogs across the river, who have set off others along the Thimphu Expressway and so on. I imagine all across the city dogs are awake now and going berserk.

It is nearly dawn when Mal returns. The man has long gone and Cecile has barricaded herself and the children in her bedroom, assuring Mal she will ring at any further hint of trouble.

Word spreads quickly around the estate, and the next morning all the neighbours congregate at Cecile's house. She is still shaking as she tells of waking to find a man wearing a balaclava going through the chest of drawers by her bed. Seven-year-old Roos was asleep on one side of her, and baby Abel had just fallen off her breast after his 1 am feed on the other.

As she sat up, a male voice said, 'Good evening, madam.' She says she reacted instantly, launching herself out of bed and screaming at him: 'Who are you? What are you doing?' He was polite, she tells us in disbelief. Apologetic, even. Only a Bhutanese burglar would be polite, she says, with a trace of her old humour.

The rest is mostly a blur. She remembers racing past her other daughter, five-year-old Willjemin, asleep in bed; smashing the glass in the front door, blood on her hands; standing on the front lawn, screaming, 'There is a man in my house! Help me!' and her angst when no-one came. Not the family of six from Uzbekistan who live just 10 metres away, or the Indian couple about 30 metres away, or her Bhutanese landlords about 50 metres away. Not us, on the other side of the corn patch. Only the dogs paid any attention. We all feel shamed.

Cecile is a strong woman, confident and capable, and it's disturbing to see her so fragile and vulnerable. Every few minutes her face crumples and the tears flow. Then she pulls herself together. She won't ring Hans. His work is important and he needs to finish what he is doing.

As the morning wears on, the children go to school and the maids arrive. Cecile's Bhutanese landlords order bars on all her windows, and in the meantime a carpenter fits lengths of wooden dowel into each window track, stopping them from being forced open. Four police officers come to her house. They take out a large magnifying glass and take it in turns to peer closely at the spot where they believe the intruder climbed in the window. We watch their Sherlock Holmes performance, transfixed. It's not making Cecile feel any safer, but it does make her smile.

The intruder stole a Bhutanese amulet and a silk shawl, which he dropped on his way down the road. While the crime was petty, it shatters the calm of Tashi Pelkhil, and its effects ripple across the estate.

The army guards are in trouble for slacking off on sentry duty when the General is away, and are told to increase their night patrols.

Roos tells her captivated class that she had a burglar in her bedroom. Other students start sleeping in their parents' bed, scared the burglar will pick their home next. Jesper orders an expensive alarm system from Denmark. In my sleep I scream out for Kathryn and before Mal's eyes are open he is out of bed, checking on her.

We offer Cecile our spare room but she declines. Until Hans returns, she continues to sleep with all three children in her room, the door locked and a chair wedged under the handle.

All that Cecile can say for sure is that the burglar was a man. Overnight, every man visiting the estate becomes a suspect, and it becomes obvious that every man *feels* like a suspect. The half-a-dozen Indian workers camping in bamboo huts near the bridge stop meeting our gaze. We used to cheer them on when they played soccer on their Sundays off, but that friendliness dissipates and they keep to themselves. The maids no longer feel safe walking up the road to catch the bus when they work late. Some of the harmony we took for granted has been lost.

After a couple of weeks, Cecile says she thinks she knows the identity of the intruder, and so does the man in the corner shop across the bridge. They whisper the name of their suspect to each other and both nod. The police, however, find no evidence. Hans returns and life goes on at Tashi Pelkhil, but with a new awareness among residents.

The Uzbeki family is horrified that they are Cecile's closest neighbours and slept through the incident. The wife, Lola, who has refused months of afternoon-tea invitations from Cecile, starts dropping by to check on her. They are a devout Muslim family and, apart from a nod if we pass each other on our evening stroll, they have mostly kept to themselves. That changes. A 15-year-old daughter we didn't know existed appears at our door with a plate of spicy shredded meat and rice. Lola seeks out Mal for advice on their hot-water geyser. Her husband works for the United Nations and wouldn't have a clue about such things, she says. Next thing I know, Mal is taking his toolbox over to the Uzbeki home and Lola is sending us regular food platters.

The taciturn estate manager, who lives with his children in a log cabin and has always ignored us, starts to smile when he sees us. This odd community, with its wealthy Bhutanese land owners alongside workers and expats from wildly different cultures, bonds a little bit closer. It is ironic that at the same time our little village seems scarier, it also becomes friendlier.

Driving to work, I look more closely at the shutters on the shop windows. They are made of steel. Nearly every shopfront in the main street of Norzin Lam has one. I wonder why I hadn't noticed that before.

I listen with new awareness at *Bhutan Observer* news conferences as the reporters tell of knife wounds treated every night at Thimphu hospital, the family that was robbed of rice and cooking utensils by armed intruders, and handbags being stolen through bars on ground floor windows in the next suburb.

Thimphu has a crime problem. It's not New York, but it's a problem all the same.

6

The Biggest Story Not Reported

To commemorate 100 years of monarchy, *Bhutan Observer* runs an essay-writing competition for students, and Phuntsho asks me to join the judging committee. I start to make excuses. I know little of Bhutanese history and can't read Dzongkha. She says half the essays are in English and it won't hurt me to learn about their royal family. She is a smiling steamroller: it's impossible to say no.

The judging panel – comprising the three section editors and me – meet on a Saturday in the boardroom. I walk into a heated discussion: the rules published in the newspaper said there would be only one winner, but the editor of the Dzongkha edition argues that the languages can't be compared, so we will have to choose two winners.

I don't understand the problem. Isn't the winner the one who writes the best essay about the Kings? What does it matter if they write it in Dzongkha or English?

The arts editor, who was raised in a Dzongkha-speaking home, explains that it wouldn't be fair. Dzongkha has five words for compassion and five words for knowledge, and the language is more internal than English, which revolves around the external. In expressing the sublime qualities of the Kings, a student fluent in Dzongkha can write more profoundly and with more nuance than a student who uses English. They have an enormous advantage.

That shuts me up. I ponder it for the rest of the morning. Five words for compassion? How can you parse the meaning of compassion into five different slivers? Why do they need to? Does it follow then that Dzongkha-speaking people understand knowledge and compassion better than we English speakers? I start to become conscious of connections between culture and language that I hadn't considered before.

The judges decide that, to be fair to the students writing in English, who are at a disadvantage with just one word for compassion, we will award two winners – one in each language.

Judging the essays gives me a crash course in the history of the Bhutanese royal family. By the time I leave the room some five hours later, I've read hundreds of essays and learned about the achievements of the Kings. It is a strangely humbling experience.

I'm as cynical about royalty as any journalist who has spent time covering the scandals of the British royal family. Years spent working on Fleet Street newspapers and Australian women's magazines crushed any faith I might've had in the monarchy. But I find myself developing a grudging respect for the Bhutanese Kings. They were mavericks, each of them, and moved the country forward regardless of what was going on elsewhere in the world.

The First King united the country. Centuries after the Zhabdrung had died and Bhutan had gone back to being a mess of warring tribes, he brought peace and encouraged trade within Bhutan by improving transport and communication. He also established education outside the monasteries.

The Second King opened medical clinics and signed the first treaty with India. He repaired infrastructure, including bridges, monasteries and temples.

The Third King was educated in England from the age of 15, and opened Bhutan a little to the outside world. During his reign, the country joined various international organisations, including the Colombo Plan in 1962 and the United Nations in 1971. He signed up India to pay for roads and telephone lines. He also abolished serfdom and capital punishment, and established an independent judiciary.

The Fourth King gave the world Gross National Happiness, and introduced democracy to his country.

Schoolchildren learn about the royal family in class. Kathryn can recite the full names of all four Queen Mothers in order of seniority, using a sing-song chant Mal made up to help her remember them all. Ashi Dorji Wangmo Wangchuck, Ashi Tshering Pem Wangchuck, Ashi Tshering Yangdon Wangchuck and Ashi Sangay Choden Wangchuck. At the end of the year she makes a card for the Fifth King, decorating it with hearts and bells and wishing him a 'Merry and Happy new year'.

Despite being the most important people in the country, the royal family rarely make it into any of the newspapers. The Fourth King and Fifth King are only covered when they attend an official function to which newspapers have been invited. Mostly it's a photo opportunity and the palace provides the pictures, while the stories reproduce their speeches in their entirety. I ask Needrup what would happen if the palace didn't like something in a story. Would someone phone him? He shrugs. He doesn't know, as it's never happened. He would never publish something the palace wouldn't like – not out of fear but because, like any good editor, he knows his community. Censorship doesn't come from the top; rather, it comes from the bottom. Respect and reverence for the royals is hardwired into every reporter, editor, reader and person on the street. It's part of their cultural fabric. Bhutanese deference means ordinary people won't look their royals in the eye. Drivers have been known to plough into rice paddies when they meet a royal car on the road and lower their gaze.

The royal family seldom comes up in news conferences. There is no media coverage of a car accident involving one of the Fifth King's brothers, a handsome young prince-about-town. Nor is it mentioned when Bollywood's hottest actress flies in for the coronation or when a beautiful young Bhutanese woman starts to accompany the Fifth King to functions. The palace doesn't volunteer photos or information on who she is, and the newspapers don't ask. No scandal, no speculation, no reducing the sacredness of the Druk Gyalpo to ordinariness. The people most emphatically do not want that.

But it's not just any potential scandal that goes unreported. Even the Fifth King's good works are mostly ignored. Some of the stories I hear from expats or in Bhutanese homes suggest the King is rather good at his job. He appears to be a genuinely kind man. It's just not reported in the newspapers.

Although single, the Fifth King adopted two sons, both poor orphans with special needs, and they live with him. One of them, Ugyen, is at Rosemary's School with Kathryn. He wears thick glasses and appears a happy, well-cared-for child, with his own devoted attendant to take him to and from school. When the Fifth King is out of Thimphu, the attendant comes to the school's performance of *The Jungle Book* to cheer him on and take lots of photos.

I hear from expat friends about an Austrian doctor in a country clinic who had to tend to a royal uncle after he fell into a rock crusher. It was a horrific accident and the man was dead when he was brought in, but Dr Susan was told to try to save him anyway. Knowing it was futile, she went through the motions of an emergency resuscitation. The sterile packets she opened were mouldy, and when she turned to look for a nurse there was no-one. Unbeknown to her, the Fifth King had turned up unexpectedly and, shocked by the sight of him, the staff had fled. The Fifth King had been visiting flood victims nearby when he heard of the accident. Seeing that Dr Susan was alone, he offered to help her clean the body, which she said was a messy job. When they finished she thanked him, saying her adult sons wouldn't have been able to perform such a gruesome task. He replied humbly that it was the least he could do. Then, just as quietly as he appeared, he slipped away. No fuss, no fanfare and, even when I tell the reporters about it, no interest from the newspaper. They are not surprised or excited by stories about the Fifth King performing good works. That's what he does. Such stories are not newspaper fodder; they circulate by word of mouth.

Kuensel was invited to report on a royal visit to the east, providing a rare occasion to read about a personal interaction between the Fifth King and his subjects. In a remote valley the Fifth King met a woman who had been ostracised because it was believed she was 'a poisoner'. Villagers thought they would die if they took food or drink from her hands. The 49-year-old woman accepted this as her karma.

According to *Kuensel*, the Fifth King was warned to stay away from her. Instead, he sought her out and embraced her. He drank two cups of *ara* (rice-brewed alcohol) from her hands, and the rest of his entourage lined up to do the same. The Fifth King told her to tell the world that she had served him in person and that stories of her poisoning others were baseless. Her life changed: from that moment she was welcomed back into her community.

The way the Bhutanese speak about their Kings, they sound like a cross between living gods and benevolent uncles who are very much part of their lives. When Phuntsho speaks of the Fourth King, her voice changes and she gets misty-eyed. She feels she has known him all her life. When he announced he was handing power over to a democratically elected government, and the crown to his son, she was devastated. It was a seismic shift of her worldview, and everyone else's in Bhutan. But his wisdom is absolute. She respects the new King and is ready to become devoted to him. No question.

The Kings also provide a sort of royal largesse, solving their subjects' problems in a uniquely Bhutanese way. The Fifth King criss-crosses the country giving *kidu*, which is translated as 'royal prerogative'. It can be given in the form of money, land or authorisation for something. In effect it means he will use his considerable powers to help where he can. To farmers who have suffered as a result of land redistribution or a road going through their orchard, he has granted *kidu* in the form of money. To the media, in recognition of the difficulties they face through inexperience, he gave *kidu* by establishing and funding the Bhutan Media Foundation to offer training programs and scholarships, and by sponsoring newspaper subscriptions for all schools.

After his coronation, the Fifth King announces he intends to personally meet every one of his subjects, and he sets himself an exhausting schedule. He travels to the most remote corners, often walking for days through jungle and snow, sleeping rough, to hear firsthand the problems of his people. Often he drags along one or more of his brothers and sisters. And where he can, he grants *kidu*.

His father set the example of being accessible and granting *kidu*. After the Fourth King returned to Bhutan from England to take the throne at the age of 17, he never left the country again, except for a trip to India. Once a week he threw open the doors of the palace for people to come and tell him their problems. It was through these open days that the Fourth King met his four wives. The story goes that the eldest of the sisters came to tell him of her family, whose potato farm was struggling. He listened, gave some form of *kidu* and invited her to come back to tell him how her family was doing. Over time a friendship developed, and at some point she brought her sisters along to meet the King. I don't know what happened after that, but somehow or other they all got married. It's not in the history books or referred to in the newspapers, and there is only so much gossip about their Kings that the Bhutanese will share with a foreigner.

*

Bhutan Observer's special coronation edition is a huge success. The Bhutanese are mesmerised by the pictorial wraparound, the country's first: eight glossy pages featuring the Fourth King, the Fifth King and a rare treat – the rest of the royals. A series of photos shows the four Queen Mothers standing in line, laughing with the Gandhi family. Readers pore over every detail, admiring the Queen Mothers' glamorous *kiras* and elegant red coral jewellery. The five princesses wear jewelled Alice headbands in their hair – a new style statement that will immediately be adopted by the fashion-conscious young women of Thimphu. Even the Fourth King's much-loved sister Ashi Dechen Wangmo Wangchuck is photographed. She hasn't been seen in public for years, spending her time in solitary retreat in a monastery near the border of Bhutan and Tibet. Her elaborate *kira* dispels rumours that she has become a nun. Clearly, she hasn't taken robes and shaved her head.

To see the royals captured so informally is intriguing to readers. The edition sells out within a matter of days, their best-selling issue ever, with a circulation of around 9,000. National distribution in this mountainous terrain is usually a problem, but not this week. People in Thimphu buy extra copies to send to their families in remote villages. Whether the villagers can read the stories or not, they will proudly tape the pictures to their walls.

7

The Light on the Hill

Phuntsho gives her staff a day off to thank us for the late hours we put in during the coronation celebrations, so Mal and I hike up the mountains that ring the city to a popular picnic spot by the BBS TV transmission tower. From here we can see into the next valley and glimpse the one beyond. The view sweeps across Tashichhodzong, a massive fortress built by Zhabdrung Rinpoche that houses both monks and the civil service, then over the modest palace of the Fifth King, along the meandering Wang Chhu river, across squat city buildings, and all the way to the foothills, where the Fourth King's royal compound nestles in groves of cypress and pine.

The tiered golden roofs of the palaces of the Queen Mothers glisten in the sun. It must be an auspicious day because we can hear the sound of rhythmic drums and discordant trumpets drifting across the clear air. Monks are conducting a *puja* at one of the royal homes.

The transmission tower is much like any other and not the reason that anyone – apart from technicians – comes up here. The attraction is this view and the unique ambience, partly created by the forest of prayer flags that flap in the wind, setting up a baritone vibration that goes right through the body.

Joseph Campbell writes in *The Power of Myth* that the tallest buildings reveal what dominates a society. In a medieval town it was the cathedral spire reflecting the supremacy of the church. In an 18th-century town it was the political palace, the houses of parliament. In a modern industrial society the tallest buildings are offices, the centres of economic life. In Bhutan, mobile-phone and television transmission towers are edging their way up the mountains, but prayer flags and temples still soar above them all.

Mal and I hike up the steep path, past the transmission tower, to the temple along the ridge at the top. We know nothing about it except that it is there, which seems a good enough reason on this sunny, dry winter afternoon.

It is an uneven, winding path, and after an hour or so we reach the temple. While we are catching our breath, a wooden door creaks open and two monks appear, nodding and smiling to us as they walk to an outhouse. It is their laundry and toilet. We're embarrassed to have encroached on their space and start to move away. Just then, a third monk appears.

He is young, perhaps in his mid twenties, with a round, pleasant face. He greets us in tentative English. It appears he wants to invite us in, but only if that's what we would like. We don't want to intrude, and the three of us smile and demur, the dance of polite strangers. Somehow, without actually agreeing, we end up following him through the wooden door in the wall, across a lawn where kitchen utensils are drying in the sun, and into a tiny courtyard. He explains that five monks are doing a three-year retreat here.

Mal starts to back away, apologising for disturbing them. The monk looks distressed. 'No, no. Please. If you would like to come in, you are welcome.'

Leaning against a wall is a ladder made from a thick tree trunk with hand-carved steps. At the top is the altar room. Like everything else in this perfectly formed temple, it manages to be both small and grand at the same time. The row of Buddhist statues towers above us, filling the room – Buddha, Guru Rinpoche, Amitabha, Manjushri and Zhabdrung Rinpoche. Their faces glow in the flickering light cast by hundreds of butter lamps. The monk tells us that behind an ornate screen threaded with white scarves is Tara, the female emanation of Buddha. She is the protector of the temple and completely hidden from view.

There is just enough room in front of this imposing line-up of statues, each up to two metres tall, for the five monks to sit.

The monk introduces himself as Yeshe. He explains the temple is called Chhokhortse Gompa. It is 3,010 metres above sea level and was built in 1345, centuries before Thimphu became Bhutan's capital. He invites us for tea. We follow him back down the ladder, across the courtyard – a distance of just six steps – and climb another hand-carved tree trunk to his quarters. He ushers us through a small room with a gas ring and groceries, and we enter his bedroom. It is so small that Mal and I sit shoulder to shoulder on the single mattress jammed against the wall. This is where he sleeps and meditates, for hours at a time, day after day. A low wooden bench acts as his table and stores his prayer books. The walls are covered in *thangkhas*, ornate wall hangings of Buddhist deities.

In the wall beside his mattress is a window, which he slides open. It looks over the courtyard, and if we angle our heads we can see a breathtaking view across the valley of Thimphu.

Yeshe explains the practices that he is doing, and that his day starts at 3 am. I ask how cold it is at that hour. He says that when he wakes, the glass of water beside his bed is frozen.

He digs out a plastic sleeve of photographs that show his family, other monks and a younger, bearded version of himself. It was taken on the day he finished his last three-year retreat. His voice is wistful.

'That was a happy day?' asks Mal.

He grins, his face so open and full of joy that it feels good just to look at him. Those three years were the best of his life, he says, and that's why he's back to do it again.

On his table is a booklet in Tibetan. It is advice from a great master about how to treat all beings with generosity. From the lowly to the highest born, everyone deserves respect and compassion. He explains it is not part of his retreat but something extra he reads. He considers our visit a blessing as it is providing him with the opportunity to be generous. He bustles about at his gas ring making tea, and produces a tin of biscuits. They are obviously a treat, but he is pleased when we both take one.

He chats about his retreat. In a few days the temple will be sealed and then things will start in earnest for the five monks. The hours of meditation will increase. Four sessions a day, starting at 3 am and ending at 9 pm. An attendant will hike up and down the mountain every few days to get food supplies from Thimphu. He will be the only person to pass through the high walls for the next three years, three months and three days.

The five monks won't talk to each other, directing all their energies on focusing their minds. Nor will they shave or cut their fingernails.

Yeshe explains the pastel-coloured dough figures on his altar, which are moulded into geometric shapes, and the cage surrounded by blood-red spikes on a low table. These strange artefacts are his armoury. While meditating and reciting his prayers, he performs elaborate and violent visualisations of scary deities to slay his ego. While the modern world goes about its business, he will be alone inside these very close walls, hour after hour, wrestling with his mind in a major battle. For all his mild manner and boyish smile, this is not a pursuit for the faint-hearted. Or the weak-willed.

We say our goodbyes, wishing him well. What do you say to a young man with a happy, shining face, who is about to be sealed up for three years to draw out and then fight his demons?

When we tell him we will be thinking of him he is pleased and says he will remember us in his prayers. Our last sight of him is that broad, open grin – and the realisation that he is looking forward to the next three years with relish. I don't know anyone who looks forward to a day in the office with that kind of enthusiasm.

We climb down the mountain, through the forest of prayer flags, past the transmission tower, and descend into the valley. Now that we know it is there, we realise Yeshe's little temple is visible from just about everywhere in Thimphu. We see it from Tashi Pelkhil, my office, the new children's playground by the river, the traffic-heavy main street of Norzin Lam. Wherever we go, we know that little flash of white amid the dense dark green high on the ridge is the ancient temple where Yeshe is doing battle.

He is part of Bhutan's hidden, esoteric, tantric face. In the West the word 'tantra' has come to carry New Age and sexual connotations. In the practice of Vajrayana Buddhism, however, it is more complex – and interesting – as explained by Chogyam Trungpa Rinpoche in *Cutting through Spiritual Materialism.*

More than 30,000 Bhutanese are monks or nuns, living in monasteries. A further 15,000 are lay monks, or *gomchen.* The *gomchen* tradition is specific to Vajrayana Buddhism, and brings the esoteric practices of tantra out of the high-walled monasteries and into the lay community. Literally translated, *gomchen* means 'great meditator'. They study and meditate as vigorously as monks and nuns, undertaking three-year retreats like Yeshe. But unlike monks and nuns, they can marry, have families and live in the villages, where they offer spiritual guidance. They are highly accomplished and respected.

When Mal was filming *Travellers & Magicians* in 2002, half-a-dozen *gomchen* appeared in a scene. I lined up with them in the breakfast queue before they were called onto the set, and could not take my eyes off them. They each had long grey hair, wore distinctive robes and radiated charisma. They also seemed amused by everything around them.

While not all Bhutanese want to embrace such a spiritual life, the whole society supports those who do – not only in terms of infrastructure and material support but also, and more importantly, through cultural affirmation and respect. You won't find Bhutan's wayward youths throwing stones at a yogi's retreat hut. This form of religious practice provides the philosophical backbone and cultural values that underpin everything about this society. And it begins to explain some of the absenteeism at *Bhutan Observer.*

The arts editor takes off whenever an important lama is giving teachings, and people work around his absences. Another becomes unavailable when his father-in-law dies and it is his responsibility to co-ordinate 49 days of mourning for the extended family.

Phuntsho puts aside her many important projects during the week that 12 monks perform *pujas* at her apartment. Her family, like most in Thimphu, have *pujas* performed at least once a year. She spends days preparing for it, explaining to me the logistics of supplying a dozen adult men with three suitably hearty meals a day, endless tea and the various offering substances they need (such as rice and fresh fruit) for each stage of the *puja*, which will be performed in the living room of her small apartment. But two days after they start, some of them have to go to Punakha to perform a *puja* for the Fifth King. They return to Phuntsho only to be called out to the Queen Grandmother. Monks are always in high demand, particularly those who have done three-year retreats for certain deities associated with specific practices. When Phuntsho finally returns to the office she is exhausted.

Respect for the spiritual underpins and permeates every aspect of Bhutanese life. It always takes precedence over getting the newspaper out.

8

Happy, Happy, Happy

Rabi Dahal is the sort of reporter that editors want in their newsroom. If he is sent somewhere to do one story, he comes back with five. While most of the reporters manage three or four stories a week, he averages around ten. In his downtime, he runs the newspaper website and helps with advertising. He is a one-man network, always ready with ideas and enthusiasm. Rival news organisations have tried to poach him, offering almost twice his salary at *Bhutan Observer*, but he is not motivated by money. He enjoys his job. He explains to me one day that the most important thing for job satisfaction is that your employer matches your own philosophy of life. He shares the vision of Tenzin, Phuntsho and Needrup, for a socially responsible newspaper that will help the Bhutanese transition to democracy. He's very at home at *Bhutan Observer*.

Rabi returns from a trip to the far northeast with a head full of stories. He travelled with officials from the Gross National Happiness Commission (GNHC) who were crossing the country to check on the happiness levels of the population. In the 2005 census, 96.4 per cent declared themselves to be 'happy' or 'very happy'. Only 3.5 per cent said they were 'not very happy'. Rabi followed as the survey team walked up mountains and through forests, going from village to village, asking people if they were happy and recording their responses in official ledgers. Faced with these important men from government, the people unanimously agreed that they were happy.

But Rabi, remembering his own childhood growing up in a poor village in the south, was not convinced officials were getting the full picture.

'I suspected they were just being obedient Bhutanese, telling the authorities what they wanted to hear, afraid of getting into trouble. So I went back and asked them if they were happy. I said, "I am a newspaperman, you can tell me the truth." They said, "Of course we are not happy. We don't have enough food to eat."'

He recounts the story to Needrup, Phuntsho and me as we sit in her office, drinking tea. Rabi tells of a woman he interviewed who was so poor she could barely afford food but nonetheless gave eggs to a GNHC official.

Needrup and Phuntsho are visibly moved. Their hearts are back in their own villages, with their families. They understand exactly why the elderly woman would do that.

Phuntsho's eyes fill with tears. 'They are so innocent,' she says.

She and Needrup tell Rabi he must write about his trip, exactly as he saw it, for the newspaper. And he does. Beautifully. He starts his piece by saying: 'My visit to Ungar in Lhuentse was one of the best experiences of my journalistic life.'

> During my visit to Ungar, I observed that the people there were only concerned about eking out a mere existence. Their concern was about food, shelter and survival. They struggled endlessly. For them, it was simply what life meant.
>
> Coming from a similar community, I have come to realise that it is a pity that these poor people are burdened with mere reasons for survival rather than contributing to nation building as equal

> partners with their fellow-citizens. Their common parlance is, 'We are happy as we are' while they hardly have any reason to be happy … Indeed, the truth is, they aren't happy. They suffer a food shortage for at least six months in a year. Many of them are indebted to financial institutions. An old woman told me that she couldn't pay off her debt even if she 'piled life upon life'.
>
> Marauding wild animals ravage their crops every season leaving them with little of the little they grow … There are no roads and electricity. They cannot send their children to school for numerous reasons. The villagers, who have resigned to their fate, say that many government officials came to their village with pen and paper, asked questions, and never returned.

The story brings a huge reaction. Thimphu readers, most of whom also have families living in villages, are deeply moved, and Needrup publishes some of their letters. A former World Bank vice-president, Mieko Nishimizu, sends an email from Japan, saying that she read the story on *Bhutan Observer*'s website and calls Rabi 'a shining journalist'.

'Real life-experience like yours is the only way to see the world through the eyes of the invisible people,' writes Nishimizu. 'It was a joy because I am convinced that good journalism, like yours, is critical.'

Even the GNHC seems pleased that Rabi has unlocked something that its own survey team was unable to. Rabi positioned the role of journalist as neutral and safe, outside the rigid social hierarchy that governs so many Bhutanese interactions. This is the independent media functioning just as the Fourth King intended – going beyond the government view. And it's *Bhutan Observer* doing what Phuntsho hoped – giving ordinary people a voice, particularly rural people. It is a wonderful moment where the best ideals of the media are demonstrated.

In the country's first media awards, a panel of judges present Rabi with the accolade of Most Valuable Story.

I understand why the story struck such a chord. Gross National Happiness must be the most discussed topic in Thimphu. The acronym GNH is used so much that it becomes a word – 'Jeenaich'.

I hear it in just about every *Bhutan Observer* news conference, if not every conversation with Phuntsho. Upholding its principles is part of the newspaper's mission statement, published on their website.

Letter writers often use it in their arguments. On the television news each night, government ministers refer to it at every opportunity. Schoolchildren write essays trying to define it. International journalists report on it, and tourists flock to Bhutan seeking to observe it. Academics give papers on it at conferences. It's considered Buddhist yet secular, applauded for being deeply profound and also criticised for being vague and woolly. But what exactly is GNH?

As with most things in modern Bhutan, it comes back to the King. The Fourth King coined the phrase and launched the concept. It is his greatest legacy. When his father died in 1972, making him the world's youngest monarch, the Fourth King already had some idea of life outside his own isolated country. He had attended a prestigious Indian college, St Joseph's, and then Heatherdown Preparatory School in Ascot, England (also attended by Prince Andrew, UK Prime Minister David Cameron and actor David Niven), before returning to Bhutan to be taught by a personal tutor from Oxford University.

In his coronation speech in 1974, the Fourth King declared: 'The most important task before us at present is to achieve economic self-reliance to ensure the continued progress of our country in the future.'

During his first few years on the throne he became concerned by what was happening in the world beyond Bhutan. He saw that development, when left unchecked, turned into consumerism. The equality sought by globalisation also caused the homogenisation of cultures. He worried that adopting similar development policies, or even allowing them to spread into his country, would undermine Bhutanese culture as well as any hope the nation had of becoming self-reliant. He began to speak about a different path to development, one based on Bhutan's own cultural values. He talked about happiness, not wealth, as the goal.

He told London's *Financial Times* in 1987: 'We are convinced that we must aim for contentment and happiness. Whether we take five years or ten to raise the per capita income and increase prosperity is not going to guarantee that happiness, which includes political stability, social harmony, and the Bhutanese culture and way of life.'

Much of this culture and way of life developed from Buddhist beliefs, which provide a fundamentally different worldview to that of Christian-based societies. In cultures based on Christian ideas, the emphasis is on the individual, which is considered a precious and unique being with a soul. Out of this, according to sociological theorist Max Weber, capitalism evolved.

Buddhism, however, doesn't focus on the individual. It is primarily concerned with the interdependence of all things: no-one and nothing exists independently of everything else. This concern with interdependence is the foundation on which Gross National Happiness was built. Karma Ura, of the Centre for Bhutan Studies, articulated the philosophy of GNH in a government paper. He wrote: 'Members of a GNH society would cultivate a third eye, which can elevate our vision beyond individual self-interest to address the happiness of all, as a collective goal ... Equity is central to GNH.'

The Fourth King's vision was for policies that, first, don't cause harm to anyone, and, second, will benefit all sentient beings. Economic growth and change are not necessarily good. They are desirable only if they meet those two criteria.

The *Financial Times* interview marked the first time he presented these ideas to the wider world, and the article covered the front page of the magazine section of its highly read weekend edition. It was a bold move by a newspaper whose readers were bankers, economists and businesspeople. At the same time the British financial establishment was reading about this novel concept, Hollywood was making the movie *Wall Street*, with Gordon Gekko (Michael Douglas) giving his famous 'greed is good' speech. The film, released in the US in December 1987, perfectly captured the economic rationalist view that prevailed in developed countries at that time. Perhaps it was because the Fourth King's vision provided such a startling contrast, a perfect bookend, that GNH got so much international attention.

The Fourth King wasn't the first to identify the limitations of a strictly economic model for measuring progress. Robert Kennedy expressed similar concerns in 1968 in a rousing speech to students at the University of Kansas: 'Too much and too long, we seem to have surrendered community excellence and community values in the mere accumulation of material things … Gross National Product … measures neither our wit nor our courage; neither our wisdom nor our learning; neither our compassion nor our devotion to our country; it measures everything, in short, except that which makes life worthwhile.'

Unlike Kennedy, however, the Fourth King had absolute power over his country and was able to implement his vision. He created an alternative measure of progress that recognised interdependence. His government established a framework of four 'pillars' of happiness: economic development, environmental preservation, cultural preservation and good governance. By changing the focus to happiness, Gross National Product became just one pillar of success, and economic development became a means rather than an end in itself.

The Fourth King gave the Centre for Bhutan Studies the task of creating metric indicators to measure the success or failure of progress under these pillars. He created the Gross National Happiness Commission, and every new policy would have to be approved by that department.

In 2008 the government further divided the four pillars into nine 'core dimensions': psychological wellbeing, time use, community vitality, culture, health, education, environmental diversity, living standard and governance.

Gross National Happiness has its critics. Mostly they argue that happiness is subjective and can't be measured, or they point to the confusion surrounding its definition. Conferences are conducted both in Thimphu and abroad to explore what it means. At the first international GNH conference, held in Thimphu in 2004, one group said happiness was the objective of GNH. Another emphasised GNH as leading to a situation where happiness may develop but it was not explicitly happiness itself. Some saw happiness as a personal matter; others, as a social condition.

Thimphu hosts its fourth GNH conference in November 2008 and interested guests fly in to share in the discussion. Mal attends each day and comes home with stories of the sessions. A Bhutanese civil servant presents graphs and charts that show women in Bhutan are significantly less happy than men. Another session reveals Thimphu valley is the most miserable region in the country.

Conversations about GNH continue all around me – in the government, among the business community, and between ordinary people working out how they should uphold GNH, which is considered part of everyone's responsibility as a Bhutanese citizen.

When I first visited Bhutan in 2002, I had no trouble with GNH. It seemed to make sense. But the more I live with it, the less I understand. The more I hear people attempting to explain it, the more slippery it becomes. Some days I think it is inspired, revolutionary even. Other days I groan inwardly at the first hint of the phrase. People can use it to beat each other up with a subtext of *I'm more 'GNH' than you.*

Often it sounds about as vague and unachievable as the ideals of democracy. While it's admirable to say that every government and community decision should be done with compassion, how do you do that and meet everyone's needs?

Some days I resent the smug superiority that can accompany the discussion around GNH. In some Bhutanese minds it encompasses everything that is good and decent, and they gave it to the world. I want to retort that they didn't invent goodness, nor do they have a monopoly on it. Vulgar as we Westerners are, we do have those values too. We call it doing the right thing or, in the Aussie vernacular, a fair go for all. Christians would say it is just being Christian. Atheists call it humanism. Enlightened businesspeople I know call it the triple bottom line. My mother called it being nice.

But all the talk of GNH provides a stark contrast to what we see on BBC, CNN and the Australian media online. On those sites terrorism, domestic politics, the financial meltdown, celebrity and sport dominate. Bhutan is blissfully uninterested in such topics, except perhaps a bit of local archery and updates on what its own government is doing. Mostly they are discussing other things, and the discussion is always framed in terms of GNH.

I don't know that I buy everything about Gross National Happiness, but I love that it is talked about endlessly. The educated Bhutanese obsess about it. They discuss it, deconstruct it and try to wrestle it to the ground. They apply it to every facet of their new democracy. They may not have achieved it, but the fact that it figures so prominently in public discussion has to be good.

9

Australian Connections

On deadline nights after working late I catch a taxi home and find that the drivers love to chat. One day a 40-year-old driver is pleased to recognise my accent. It reminds him of Miss Sarah, the pretty Australian schoolteacher he had as a boy of 12 in the eastern district of Mongar. He also remembers eating Australian-supplied food including rice, 'fish in boxes' and something that came in a tin with a kangaroo on the front. I'm astounded and delighted. This cheerful man, resplendent in a red and orange checked *gho*, with photos of two smiling children on his dashboard, was a recipient of Australian foreign aid 28 years ago.

Another time I'm greeted by a driver singing AC/DC's 1975 hit 'TNT'. They are his favourite band, and he has 80 of their 'best' tracks on a memory stick plugged into his dashboard. He is surprised to hear that the band is Australian, not American, and cranks up the volume, which we agree is the only way to fully appreciate their genius. We speed along the national highway, belting out the lyrics, detouring around the odd cow on the road, before bouncing over the little bridge into Tashi Pelkhil. I discover we live two AC/DC songs away from the office.

Australia and Bhutan have connections that are far-reaching and often unexpected. For the coronation of the Fourth King in 1974, Australia sent a fleet of Ford Falcons, Bhutan's first cars; and for the new King's coronation we gave ten new university scholarships. We helped build Paro Airport; we also sent firemen to train Bhutanese firefighters, and scientists to assist with sheep farming and controlling fruit fly. Taltarni wine from the Victorian Pyrenees is freely available. I'm told it is because of a long-standing friendship between 'Grandpa Taltarni' and the Fourth King, and the company is helping the Bhutanese establish their first vineyard. Australian tourists are plentiful, providing the fifth-highest group of visitors (including Lachlan and Sarah Murdoch, who chose the isolated country for their 1999 honeymoon).

Nearly 60 per cent of Bhutan's cabinet ministers studied at universities in Australia. The former head of the civil service, Bap Kesang, studied accounting at Macquarie University in the seventies and famously won something like $20,000 in a lottery while he was there. Dasho Pema Thinley, the Vice Chancellor of the Royal University of Bhutan, studied at the University of New England and is the head of the Australia Bhutan Friendship Association. He invites Mal and me to a dinner honouring our countries' connections, where the special guest is John McCarthy, the Australian High Commissioner in Delhi, whose territory includes Bhutan.

Mal is seated next to the Vice Chancellor, who immediately engages him in a conversation about *Travellers & Magicians.* I'm seated next to a government minister who studied in New Zealand but is representing his wife, an Australia alumna who couldn't make it. The MP is an authority on Dzongkha, which I've become endlessly fascinated by since the essay judging. He tells me that during his university years he started dreaming in English, but now that he is speaking Dzongkha in parliament all day, he has reverted to dreaming in Dzongkha. Suddenly he stops mid-sentence and, in an urgent whisper, asks who the man opposite us is. I say Mal Watson. The MP looks stunned. His eyes bulge. He whispers that he knows all about Mal Watson because he read a book written by his wife about the making of the film *Travellers & Magicians*. I start to say that I'm that author, that wife, but he's not interested. He is leaning across the table and politely interrupting to declare that Rinpoche's style is reminiscent of legendary Japanese film-maker Kurosawa. The Vice Chancellor starts nodding furiously and it becomes apparent that these two are old friends and have dissected the film together before – they are mad film buffs. Mal starts to agree about Kurosawa and the two of them look like they could devour him.

The former deputy prime minister of Australia Tim Fischer holds a unique position in Bhutan, nominated by former prime minister Kevin Rudd as 'special envoy'. I'm told that Tim is one of the few people in the world who within a day of arriving in Thimphu can arrange a meeting with the Fourth King, the Fifth King *and* the Prime Minister.

Mal and I meet Tim when he brings a busload of Australian tourists through Thimphu. These trips are part of his strategy to build bonds between people in the two countries. He believes personal relationships can change the world. Megan Ritchie, our Australian neighbour, invites his whole tour group – and us – for a traditional Bhutanese feast at her home. Tim is a polymath with the energy of ten men. His 'hobbies' include making podcasts about trains for the ABC, writing books about rural Australia, campaigning for greater national recognition of war hero General John Monash, and all things Bhutanese. He is also the only person I've met who shares Mal's interest in the adventures of British explorer Francis Younghusband, who, according to legend, rode into Tibet with a falcon on his wrist. While Tim's tour group line up at the buffet, he and Mal drift off to a corner, mutually delighted to discover a fellow Younghusband enthusiast.

During this visit Tim is also finishing a book on Bhutan he has been writing with local historian Tshering Tashi. *Bold Bhutan Beckons: Inhaling Gross National Happiness* recounts controversial periods from Bhutan's history that haven't been written about before, including the assassination of Bhutan's prime minister in 1964, which is still a touchy subject involving high-profile families. I think that these two men – an outsider of Tim's standing and the very well-connected Tshering – are the only ones who could write such a book. Tim tracked down the daughter of the British judge brought out to conduct an independent trial on the grisly death. Bhutan has few history books and Tshering and Tim plan to give four copies to each school in the kingdom. I ask Tim if I can interview him about the book for *Bhutan Observer*. He says yes, but trying to pin him down is like trying to catch a mosquito, so I join his bus tour for a morning as they drive to a monastery on the edge of Thimphu.

Tim is the consummate tour guide, standing at the front of the bus and pointing out sites of interest. His knowledge of Bhutanese history is impressive and he is a great storyteller. He tells me he started visiting the country in 1983 after reading Hollywood actress Shirley MacLaine's book *Don't Fall off the Mountain*, which included a dramatic account of being held under house arrest during a visit to Bhutan in 1965. In the eighties MacLaine was dating the Australian leader of the Opposition, Andrew Peacock, and Tim says he thought that the best way to gain favour with 'the boss' was to read his girlfriend's book.

Tim was captivated by her descriptions of a hidden Himalayan kingdom. Since then he has been a regular visitor to Bhutan, bringing his wife, Judy, and their two sons, and becoming a close friend to the Fourth King as well as an informal adviser to the government. During his 20 years representing Australia on various matters in Beijing, Tim always spoke up for Bhutan's interests, particularly the ongoing border disputes. He says the Chinese came to expect it, and would open every meeting with an update on Bhutan 'just to get it out of the way'.

Another friend to Bhutan is Catherine Harris of the Harris Farm grocery chain. Catherine is Australia's Honorary Consul of Bhutan, and the family home in Sydney's inner west operates like an unofficial hotel for delegates. According to Cathy, the family's long association started in the 1980s, when Harris Farm was just one shop. A Bhutanese farmer on a visit to Sydney's vegetable markets asked her husband, David, for advice about harvesting mandarins. In Bhutan, he explained, farmers often were attacked by tigers. David didn't think he could help with that problem but invited him home for dinner, and the Harris family has been helping Bhutanese farmers ever since. In the 2000 Sydney Olympic Games, Cathy marched with Bhutan's team of two archers, wearing a *kira* in the team colours and waving a Bhutanese flag. Mal and I catch up with them in Thimphu when they are here on official business. While Cathy is in meetings, David is quietly investigating whether refrigerated warehouses in strategic rural locations might help farmers.

Christmas comes, and while the Bhutanese mostly ignore it, there are enough European expats in Thimphu for the excitement to build. I cut a Christmas tree out of cardboard and stick it to the wall. We make decorations from pictures cut out of Indian magazines. Kathryn adds a toilet roll that she decorated at Cecile and Hans's house, which brings a certain panache.

A Danish couple throws a traditional Danish tree-decorating party in their grand home high above Thimphu. We join their 20 or so guests sitting on the floor drinking gluhwein, and making elaborate paper ornaments of stars and angels. The Danish men are right into it and one explains he has been doing this since he was a child. They tell us how much they like Prince Frederik's Australian wife and we feel ridiculously gratified. After a few gluhweins, we're merrily toasting 'our' Mary and 'our' Fred, as if we're now one big happy family, somehow all related because two people, whom none of us have ever met, got married.

As we finish each paper ornament, we attach it to a huge pine tree in the living room. Dozens of little candles are dotted all over its branches, with a bucket of water at hand for when the tree catches alight – which happens in about three minutes. Then we are invited to hold hands, sing 'O Tannenbaum', the Danes' version of 'O Christmas Tree', and dance around the tree. Each nationality is asked to step up and sing a Christmas carol from their country. Mal slips out the back door with a Bhutanese friend, who also has no desire to sing and hold hands, leaving me and Megan to give a rendition of 'Waltzing Matilda' and shuffle around the smoking tree. I can't help wondering if this is what our Mary is doing tonight in Copenhagen.

Megan and her Bhutanese husband, Thinley, host Christmas lunch for about 40. A former academic and tourism executive, Megan now heads up the Bhutan office of Dutch aid organisation SNV, making her one of the most important people in Thimphu. She was one of the select 70 VVIPs to join the royal family *inside* the sacred chamber for the King's coronation. Her working days are spent improving life in poor communities and being feted by government ministers. For her birthday the Fifth King sent his driver to deliver to her a bottle of French champagne and a massive chocolate cake. But she is a country girl from rural New South Wales at heart and invites all the expats to bring a plate, which ensures a multicultural feast. Mal cooks two huge pots of red Thai beef curry with enough chilli to impress Megan's in-laws, who come back for seconds, thirds, fourths, and then just finish it off. Mal is chuffed when they ask for his recipe.

Thinley and his father cook beef Maori-style in a *hangi*, having risen before dawn to dig a hole in the garden, fill it with burning coals, and put the meat on top, before covering it with dirt for hours of deep, slow cooking. Thinley learned the technique from Megan's brother when he took him on a recent trip to a remote community. Worried about eating uncooked pork, Megan's brother hadn't wanted to insult his village hosts by not eating, so instead he volunteered to cook a pig for the whole village. Thinley was inspired to try it, and Christmas Day is his first chance. The Danish, Dutch and Japanese stand around the earth pit watching him dig it up and marvelling at Australia's strange Christmas traditions.

The children run wild across the estate, and we tuck Kathryn into bed delirious with exhaustion. In the weeks leading up to Christmas, she had worried that Santa might get lost over the Himalayas. But he had found his way to her on Christmas morning, leaving at the foot of the bed some books and a child-sized version of the prayer wheels she had seen old women twirl at the *lhakhang*. Kathryn puts it beside her on the pillow, looking at it in wonder. 'How did he know?' she whispers. It is the highlight of my Christmas.

10

Who's Reading?

Over the Christmas and New Year period, Rosemary closes her school for a few weeks. Some students head back to Europe and others go to beach resorts in Thailand, while the Bhutanese return to their villages. Mal and I take Kathryn to India. Mal lived in Dzongsar Khyentse Rinpoche's household in Delhi for 12 years and still has a couple of boxes of belongings there, one containing his beloved espresso machine. We decide to go and get it, travelling by train, plane and car across the continent, stopping along the way at various places – Bodhgaya, Varanasi, Sarnath, Agra. India is wild, exotic and exuberant, constantly in your face. It's a kaleidoscope of experiences for a six-year-old Aussie kid to digest, and sometimes Kathryn looks dazed by the sights unfolding in front of her, especially the devastating poverty. Beggars, sightless or limbless or both, stretch their hands out to her. Some push themselves around on skateboards, bringing them to Kathryn's eye level and making it impossible for her to look away. With her pale skin and long red hair, she is like a beacon, particularly for the children, who crowd around her.

A few days after our return, I come home from work and Dolma tells me Kathryn and our Dutch neighbour Roos are 'playing being poor'. I find them sitting in our gutter, wearing old clothes, their faces smeared with dirt. They are pretending to be beggars. I guess she's processing the experiences, the way children do, but I wonder what Dolma makes of the new game.

When the school term starts up again, Kathryn throws herself back in with gusto. At night she reads to me the books that Rosemary sets for homework. They are jolly British readers about how the Pitt family survives the Second World War. *Put That Light Out* is a rousing tale of what happens when the Germans bomb Balaclava Terrace. *Careless Talk* tells of a mysterious foreigner with a moustache and a funny accent who moves into the neighbourhood. Is he a German spy? In art, they make wartime posters. *Loose Lips Sink Ships* and *Look Out, Spies About.* Hitler starts to creep into our conversations. We drive along the river, listening to Kathryn and Roos arguing in the back seat about which country Hitler invaded first.

'It was Poland,' says Kathryn.

'No, he invaded my country first,' says Roos.

It seems a surreal conversation as we bounce over our little bridge, draped in prayer flags, the sounds of a *puja* wafting along Wang Chhu river.

Kathryn thrives at the little school. I may cringe at the thought of war history invading our peaceful idyll, but she loves it, happy to be doing the same work that older children Robert and Marlin are doing. And she is especially fond of her teacher, Miss Sonam.

Teachers are revered in Bhutan, and every year on National Teachers Day the country pays tribute to them. The Bhutanese rate education highly: the educated class in this country has perhaps more PhDs per head of population than anywhere else in the world. All government ministers and top civil servants must have at least a bachelor's degree, but preferably a master's or PhD from an international university.

Bhutan Observer willingly sponsors two of its most experienced and capable reporters to do masters' degrees at a Thailand university. The newspaper continues to pay their wages for the two years they are out of the office, and in return the reporters commit to five years' work for the company.

Needrup and a senior reporter have their sights set on masters' courses at Australian universities. Phuntsho supports them. She knows it will bring respect to the newspaper. Even though they are short-staffed and the cost is huge, she believes it is worth the investment.

While one end of society is pursuing higher education, it is a different story in villages across the country. The national literacy rate is only around 56 per cent. Rural schools lack many of the basics – books, teachers, even roofs – and some families can't give their children time off, needing them to work on their farms or sell vegetables by the roadside.

For rural children to go to school, they often must travel great distances. The newspapers run heartbreaking stories of children as young as seven walking three hours a day to school, being too exhausted to learn, then walking three hours home in the evening, braving snow, mudslides, and wild animals such as bears and leopards.

To avoid such arduous and dangerous walks, some parents build makeshift homes for their children near their schools. During the school term, older siblings look after the younger ones, cooking meals and overseeing homework. It causes enormous anguish for the parents and the children.

Newspaper readers respond to these stories with letters urging the government to do more. Education is a national priority and preoccupation. It is always in the news.

The First King started Bhutan's education revolution. In 1914, while most of the world was preoccupied with the First World War, he set about introducing modern education. Before then, only monks knew how to read and write, and people outside monasteries were illiterate. The First King believed that illiteracy bred ignorance. He wanted to develop the nation and made it his first challenge to 'remove the ignorance of his people'.

He wrote to the Viceroy of India and asked him to fund Bhutanese boys at the Scottish mission school in Kalimpong, 120 kilometres away. The Viceroy agreed. Over the next ten years, 45 boys walked over high, snow-covered mountain passes to and from Kalimpong. The King also opened a school in the country's west with teachers from the Church of Scotland mission, and in 1915 he opened a royal school for the Crown Prince and some children of people serving in the royal court. By 1920, Bhutanese boys had started going to Indian universities.

The King first wanted teachers, then medical doctors and veterinarians. Next he wanted students trained in forestry and mining, to develop the nation's resources. At that time the people also faced many hardships from a lack of roads: it took a farmer 21 days to traverse the country east to west. Thus, the King sent the following batch of students to become engineers to build roads, and to harness the great rivers of Bhutan for hydro-electricity.

He also sent two boys to learn printing. 'A printing press is a necessity for carrying on the organisation of the country under the new conditions and of supplying the necessary educational apparatus,' he said.

The First King's plan was for those boys to spearhead the process of nation building. And they did. A few generations on and Bhutan provides its own education and medical care, and the country has a forestry industry. The Bhutanese mine cement, coal, dolomite, gypsum and limestone, as well as produce hydropower. A highway connects Bhutan from east to west. And the country has a number of printing presses, producing educational materials and servicing the growing newspaper industry.

*

Even among the educated classes, however, few read newspapers for enjoyment. While *Kuensel* has been around for more than 30 years, and has grown from a record of government events to a lively, critical newspaper, its readership is mainly upper-level government employees. For many, reading newspapers is seen as work, something you do as part of your government job or because your university lecturer makes you. Why else would you read one? Bhutanese children don't grow up seeing newspapers being read by their parents, or even sold from street corners and shop counters. They are found mostly in the offices of government officials.

The director of Bhutan's media regulation agency tells me he doesn't read *any* newspapers. 'I would like to hire someone to do that,' he grumbles. 'The rest of us are too busy.'

I'm shocked. The university-educated head of the media regulation agency doesn't read the newspapers over which he is watchdog? He doesn't consider it necessary for his job? This is the challenge facing the newspapers. While the industrialised world struggles with print media losing readers to the internet, the majority of Bhutanese have yet to discover newspapers – what they do, why they might be useful or enjoyable, or how they might contribute to democracy.

BBS radio reaches most corners of the kingdom, playing news and Bhutanese music. It is cheap, immediate and doesn't require literacy. Farmers and yak herders stream it through their mobile phones. BBS television brings images of the Kings into homes throughout the country. It also shows traditional dancing, as well as any news from the government. Why would you waste Nu.10 (A$0.27) on a newspaper?

Needrup tells me that none of his university peers read newspapers now that they don't have to. His extended family, back in his home village, has no idea what he does as editor-in-chief of *Bhutan Observer.* The family watches BBS TV at a neighbour's home and listens to the radio. They have heard of *Kuensel*, but don't really understand what it does. Newspapers are a mystery, another of those new-fangled foreign things that just aren't relevant to their lives. Newspapers exist on the periphery of society.

With such a lack of interest from the public, it is not surprising that many shops don't see the point in stocking newspapers. They take up space and provide a profit of just Nu.1 (A$0.03) per copy. Among those shopkeepers who do stock newspapers, few understand the news business. Often, the latest edition is mixed in with a pile from last week.

There is also a lack of interest in journalism jobs, which makes finding staff difficult. In developed nations, working in the media is seen as an exciting career and university graduates vie for limited places at news organisations. In Bhutan, however, the media business is viewed with suspicion. Most parents prefer their children to find a job in the civil service, which is seen to be protective, part of an extended Bhutanese family. Such a job provides security and prestige, especially compared with the uncertainties of newspapers, an unfamiliar private industry.

For her interview at *Bhutan Observer*, reporter Tandin Pem had to sneak out of the house without her father knowing. The very capable advertising director, 24-year-old Gopal Singh, is under pressure from his parents to get 'serious' about his life. In their eyes his success at the newspaper means little. It is time he finds a wife and gets a real job, one with the civil service.

But most significantly, Bhutan is traditionally an oral society. They aren't used to reading. Or writing. For the average farmer or villager, the written word is a new concept. Historically only the monks needed books – prayer books – which were written in Choekey, a variation of Tibetan.

There are about 23 official Bhutanese dialects, and around 20 years ago, the Fourth King decreed that the country needed a common language. He chose Dzongkha, a dialect from the wealthier population in the country's west. The first step was to give it a written form.

A committee of 12 eminent Bhutanese men oversaw the creation of a script and applied it to Dzongkha words. The Fourth King wanted every schoolchild to learn Dzongkha in order to encourage cultural pride and unite the country. He also wanted them to learn English, the language of the wider world. Dzongkha is still a work in progress and a source of contention among people of the east and the south. The Dzongkha scholars still disagree on aspects of the language, and few teachers are qualified to teach it.

A government minister from western Bhutan tells me he was raised speaking Dzongkha. It was his farming parents' greatest aspiration that he learn English, which 30 years ago was considered the language of the educated. The minister wants his own son, however, to learn Dzongkha, which is spoken in parliament. He reasons that the more fluent his son is in Dzongkha, the more eloquent he will be in parliament. He also sees it as the language of the future. English has dropped to second place in importance.

Phuntsho, however, grew up in the east speaking Sharchop and had to learn Dzongkha and English at school. She remembers children from the west teasing her about her accent and her way of pronouncing certain Dzongkha words. Even now, as the owner of a newspaper, and a respected person in the community, she is shy about speaking Dzongkha publicly. Her son Tsangyang has just started school and is finding communication a struggle. Like his mother, he speaks Sharchop at home but is not allowed to at school, where he must learn both English and Dzongkha, two foreign languages.

At *Bhutan Observer*, news conferences slip in and out of all three languages. Nearly all of the 50 staff were raised in homes that speak Sharchop and that's what they use to talk to each other in the office. They tell me that Sharchop, which has no written form, is simple, but Dzongkha and English are both difficult to learn. The journalists are well educated and hired for their language skills, yet they struggle with one or the other or both. It is the same in most offices around Thimphu.

Language, like everything else in Bhutan, is fluid; and reading is considered something of an oddity. It is yet to catch on in the mainstream as something one might do for pleasure or to be informed.

Kuensel quotes a local joke that if you want to keep a secret in Bhutan, write it in a book. No-one will read it.

11

Bhutanese Faces

January is the coldest month and also the driest, making winter the bushfire season. The office receptionist hands out small individual bar heaters for us to put under our desks. Still, the cold blows through the cracks between the windows and walls, and seeps up through the cement floor. I wear thermals under my thermals and huddle so closely over my heater that my long woollen skirt catches alight, leaving a decorative singe along the hem.

No matter the weather, the *gho* and the *kira* don't change. As far as I can tell, only the underwear does. Men cover up their knees, wearing long johns under their long socks. But the fashion-conscious young women such as Tandin Pem continue to wear strappy bare sandals. As I shiver next to her in a news conference, I ask if her feet are cold. She says yes, of course, and I feel stupid for asking. What's logic got to do with fashion? Young Bhutanese men wear square-toed shoes a few sizes too big and some look like Mickey Mouse, flapping up Norzin Lam. At least both sexes are suffering equally for fashion.

The *Bhutan Observer* executive is invited to a grand government reception – the launch of a comprehensive study into how media is affecting people. As it is an official government function,

Phuntsho lends me a spare *rachu*, a narrow embroidered red scarf that she tells me I must wear draped across my left shoulder, over the top of my *kira*, *toego* and *wonju*, or I won't be allowed into the government building. Needrup and the other editors wear the male equivalent, the *kabney*, a silk shawl draped from the left shoulder and twisted into a loose knot at the right hip of their *gho*. In the office, the men check each other's pleats while Phuntsho adjusts my folds and tightens my belt, before we walk the short distance to the Ministry of Information and Communications. We are shown to the grand reception hall, which is already full with newspaper owners, editors and reporters, TV and radio people, and bureaucrats. If this building burned down today, there would no longer be a media industry in Bhutan.

The *Media Impact Study 2008* is a follow-up to a 2003 study jointly conducted by Stanford University and Siok Sian Pek-Dorji, founder and head of the Bhutan Centre for Media and Democracy. For months her teams have been conducting focus groups across the country, drilling down into people's homes and thoughts.

Pek, as she is known, is a formidable analyst and one half of Bhutan's most powerful media couple. She is married to Kinley Dorji, who has recently left his post as *Kuensel* editor-in-chief to work for the Ministry of Information and Communications. Kinley was Bhutan's first journalist, one of a handful of promising young men whom the Fourth King had sent to study at foreign universities in the 1980s. Kinley went to Bathurst, Australia, and studied journalism alongside Andrew Denton and Amanda Keller. Pek was a fellow student and a former presenter on an investigative television program in Singapore. The couple returned to Bhutan, where Kinley launched *Kuensel* and Pek worked with the new Bhutan Broadcasting Service. Throughout their careers they both continued to study. Pek completed a Master of International Relations at Macquarie University, Sydney, and Kinley studied a Master of Arts in Journalism at Columbia University,

New York. They have co-presented papers at academic conferences around the world on media, ethics and democracy.

Kinley and Pek were the country's first journalists, and it seems fitting that as the media has matured in Bhutan, so have their roles. He is like the godfather of journalism, a steady hand advising government from the inside, while Pek's organisation acts as an independent overseer of the whole industry.

Pek starts her presentation by saying that in the past five years, it is as if Bhutan has been living on speed – even the rate of change itself is accelerating. A murmur of agreement goes around the room. The arrival of democracy, a new King and a burgeoning media, including television and the internet, all in such a short space of time, has left people dizzy.

In 2003, media was used for information but in 2008, she says, it has become about entertainment. While radio continues to be the most popular form of media, it is the newer forms that have caused the biggest cultural changes. At every level of society the mobile phone has become an indispensable tool, part of everyday life. Bhutanese use it mainly to talk but also to stream radio, play music, send messages, take photos and play games. Television is bringing the outside world in all its diversity and complexity into homes, from WWE wrestling (a big hit) and *Buffy the Vampire Slayer* to Korean rock music, CNN and nature documentaries. Many parents believe this exposure is good for their children, making them more confident. But overwhelmingly the Bhutanese want to see themselves on television. More Bhutanese faces, more Bhutanese stories. Nearly 40 per cent say Bhutanese television is their favourite form of media, with just 9 per cent favouring international TV – which is particularly impressive given that BBS doesn't broadcast all day and repeats its shows. Viewers also mistrust foreign television. Nearly 30 per cent said BBS TV was always believable, but just 7.5 per cent said the same about international television.

For the 10,000 internet users there is Wikipedia and more. They can find out anything they want to know at the click of a mouse. In a country with few books and even fewer libraries, this is a sudden abundance of information. Young adults working in offices in the main towns are discovering a revolutionary new way to socialise with each other: Facebook. It is also how they keep in touch with Bhutanese friends studying abroad.

And the connectivity is set to spread. The government is working to provide high-speed internet to each of the 205 *gewogs* (groups of villages) across the country. Every school, health clinic and local-government hub will be connected.

Newspapers have been the slowest to make headway. The launch of new ones means a dynamic, sometimes raucous, national public conversation is now going on, but only among the educated in Thimphu and the major cities. Rural readers say they feel left out, with one farmer commenting that because his village was never mentioned, he no longer felt part of Bhutan. Others commented that they did not like it when newspapers disagreed with each other – how could there be two sets of facts?

I feel Phuntsho nodding beside me throughout most of the presentation. The study confirms all her instincts. Bhutanese want Bhutanese voices telling Bhutanese stories.

I take home the report and digest its 1,505 pages. I sort out the parts that seem the most relevant to *Bhutan Observer* and put them into a PowerPoint presentation. During a three-day workshop with editorial, advertising and management, we unpack what Pek's findings mean for the newspaper.

Our workshop starts well. The staff are amused by the reactions of rural people to nudity on television. They knew that *Kuensel* got most of the government's advertising but are shocked at just how much – nearly half of the Nu.100 million (A$2.74 million), while the rest is divided between the other seven media organisations.

But when I get to the readership figures, they start to look miserable. *Kuensel* is the market leader with 34.7 per cent, followed by *Bhutan Times* with 21.7 per cent, and *Bhutan Observer* last at 20.9 per cent. They say the survey is no good. It cannot be true. *We can't be behind Bhutan Times. That's not possible.*

I say that the study is credible and we should not be defensive. The survey shows that the newspaper is highly respected. It just doesn't have a very high profile: many people still do not know about it. Perhaps the reason *Bhutan Times* did better has something to do with the newspaper giveaway they did in the weeks leading up to the survey. Perhaps *Bhutan Times* stands apart because it is different, not necessarily better, while *Kuensel* and *Bhutan Observer* are more alike, both more serious. Maybe *Bhutan Observer* needs to develop a personality away from *Kuensel*, to give it a point of difference.

The mood in the room lifts when I get to Pek's recommendations. Everything she says should be done is what *Bhutan Observer* is already doing. Rural stories, children's pages, no stories from the internet and more stories about Bhutan. Pek's recommendations perfectly match their vision for a socially responsible newspaper.

It takes all day to go through the study and the staff come up with lots of areas in which the paper can improve, such as finding more advertising, raising our profile among students and schools, making rural people feel more included, developing our webpage, and connecting to radio listeners. The next day, the different departments brainstorm specific ideas, with the limitations being that the paper cannot afford more staff, and any idea must maintain the values of the newspaper.

The advertising department reports back first. Their head, Gopal, starts humbly. He says the advertising department had believed that readers bought the newspaper for the advertisements, so they were disappointed to discover that only 8 per cent of readers did so.

But, he says, it has made them realise something else. If 37 per cent of people buy the newspaper for the news, then it is up to the journalists to get better news to attract more readers. Gopal says they feel that the journalists write too many negative stories. He recommends they should write softer, nicer, more positive stories, ones that make people feel good. The mood in the room plummets.

Editorial has its turn after lunch, and the political reporter strikes back, explaining what the word 'news' in *news*paper means. Softer, nicer, more positive stories, indeed! The political reporter tells the advertising department that they should concentrate on getting advertisements and leave to editorial the more *important* job of producing a credible newspaper. He speaks eloquently and the reporters nod furiously throughout.

And so it begins. The battle lines are drawn. Advertising versus editorial, just like in newspaper offices all over the world. Maybe it was inevitable, or even healthy, a sign that the two departments are taking responsibility for their own patches. But I worry that *Bhutan Observer* is starting to look a lot more like other offices I have worked in than it did a week ago. Did I do that?

When editorial and advertising aren't blaming each other, they come up with lots of good ideas: a children's page in the Dzongkha edition; citizen journalism from Bhutanese students studying abroad; branded merchandise for potential advertisers; a media kit selling the newspaper's strengths to advertisers; a business page; marketing the newspaper in cinemas; web classifieds; and so on. I type them up overnight, attaching questions to each about how to make them happen. Next morning we mix up the discussion groups – a couple of editorial with a couple from advertising and management – and this works well. They come at things differently and find opportunities for each other. It also seems to restore a sense of harmony.

*

The entrepreneurial zeal of the office spills over to home. Mal, Kathryn and I are enjoying yak burgers with chips at Thimphu's hippest eatery, The Zone, when Mal announces an idea. In his daily online reading about Mac computers and software, he has discovered a new mosaic program. It can re-create a photograph using thousands of different images. Why not make a birthday poster of the Fifth King using photos of his subjects?

Kathryn and I stare at him in admiration. It is an inspired idea. The Fifth King has been dubbed 'the people's king' because of his down-to-earth style. He did not invite any of the world's royals to his coronation, nor any leaders he did not know personally. If he had, protocol would have meant spending time with them when he really wanted to celebrate the grand occasion with his people. Thus, the only international VVIPs invited were the Indian Prime Minister, along with Sonia Gandhi and her children, who are long-time family friends. The Fifth King spent much of the three-day celebration mingling with the crowd. As he said in his coronation speech, he wants his reign to be all about the people. A poster capturing that would be brilliant.

Mal buys the mosaic software over the internet and applies it to a formal photo of the Fifth King, using his own photo collection to supply the thousands of photos. Then he brings it in to present to Phuntsho and Tenzin, explaining that *Bhutan Observer* readers could be invited to send in their photos for him to perform this computer wizardry. It would be a way for them to wish their King a happy birthday.

Mal tapes the mock-up poster to a wall in Tenzin's office, and the four of us walk towards the thousands of smiling faces, then backwards until it is the King's regal personage once more. We do it again and again, hovering at that point where the image transitions from one image to many. Mal laughs at our obvious delight. Tenzin and Phuntsho speak to each other urgently in Sharchop, then Tenzin says,

'Yes, yes, this is very good, let's do it.' But first he must seek permission from the palace. He makes an appointment and takes a printout of the mock poster with him.

Tenzin always looks dapper, but for a visit to the palace, he is resplendent in a multi-striped *gho* with his special-occasion *kabney*. My heart is in my mouth the whole time he is gone. Mal and I may have seriously misjudged this. It is not quite the royal visage on a tea-towel, but the Fifth King and his court may well see it that way.

Tenzin returns to the office very excited. He says the palace doesn't just like it, they think it is the cleverest thing that has ever been proposed by any media company.

Mal makes a television advertisement for the project on his computer and goes around the office eavesdropping on staff to find the best voices. He chooses one of the girls in advertising to voice the English version and a Dzongkha translator, who is also a famous Bhutanese movie star, for the Dzongkha version. The local youth radio station lets them record the ad in a soundproof booth.

After the advertisement goes to air, the photos start to pour in by email, mobile phone and the post. Some are even hand-delivered. There are lots of dignified, non-smiling graduation and passport photos, as well as pictures showing happy moments on picnics by rivers. One rural schoolteacher sends in photos of all his students, dozens of them. Two members of staff send in so many of themselves that we have to cull them, for fear of ending up with one whole row of reporter Rabi and another of advertising head Gopal. Mal trims, crops and edits each photo individually, then loads them into the program. It takes three all-nighters, but finally one morning I wake up to find he has finished.

He hands it over to the newspaper's graphic designer, Sushil. The car importer Zimdra agrees to sponsor the posters and he places their logo discreetly on the bottom along with the words, 'Birthday Greetings from the People'.

The finished digital file is couriered to Delhi and printed into two different-sized posters made of thick, high-quality paper, then trucked back to Thimphu. They look spectacular. Before they go on sale, Tenzin has one framed for the Fifth King and presents it to the Prime Minister in a private appointment. He takes the office photographer to record the auspicious occasion. That photo takes pride of place in his office.

The mosaic posters are a marketing hit but it takes a while before they become a financial success. The problem, as always, is distribution. There just are not enough shops to sell them, and those that do sell them do not display them well. When we can't see any posters in Thimphu's largest bookshop (there are only three), we enquire at the front desk and are shown to an out-of-the-way corner. The posters are covered in opaque plastic to 'protect' the King. Selling out may take a while.

We trek up to the ridge behind Thimphu, past the BBS tower, to Yeshe's *lhakhang* and hurl a poster over the high wall. Inside we have taped a note explaining where he can find his own face. It makes us feel good to imagine his delight.

12

The Myth of Shangri-La

One February morning we wake up to the news that Victoria, my home state, is on fire. We eat breakfast in shocked silence as we watch footage of houses exploding into flames live on BBC. Survivors and fighters tell stories of unimaginable heat. Raining fireballs. I don't remember hearing such descriptions before and feel a heavy sense of impending doom. I stream the ABC news on my computer in the office, worrying about friends who have a raspberry farm at Kinglake, an hour north-east of Melbourne. Every now and then the radio host Richard Stubbs is interrupted by news of an imminent threat to a specific community. Names that are so familiar: Marysville, Yarra Glen, Christmas Hills, Beechworth, Healesville, Yea Road. I realise people in these places are listening to the same broadcast and making life-and-death decisions about whether to stay or go. It is an eerie feeling to be so connected and yet so disconnected.

I watch through my window as five men make their way up Norzin Lam. They look strange and foreign in their *ghos* with stiff back pleats and long white cuffs. I feel a wave of homesickness. I start emailing people in Australia for news of our friends. At 4 pm I get a reply: they got out safely, but lost the farm. I remember when they planted their first raspberry vines 25 years ago. Megan starts texting me, clearly desperate with worry. Her home is in Chiltern and she has a friend in Yackandandah who just sent a text saying she is watching from her verandah the fire coming towards her.

Victoria continues to burn, and on Monday morning I sit in the news conference feeling hollow. The staff have no idea of the bushfires that have been the headlines on CNN and BBC all weekend. Of more interest to them today are traditional Bhutanese sports that are disappearing. They keep weaving in and out of Dzongkha and Sharchop, and I struggle to keep up. Someone mentions cockfighting. Is that with roosters, I ask. They fall about laughing at my ignorance. It is played between two men who each have one leg tied behind them and they hop at each other, banging bodies and heads until one falls over. *That's a sport?* Yes, and so is another game where someone drops a hanky and competitors have to do something to pick it up. I have trouble understanding much of what is said, even the bits in English. My body is here but my mind is back in Australia.

A friend emails me photos of two people she loved who died, one in the fires and one from a heart attack. I print them out and climb the 108 steps to Changangkha Lhakhang to request prayers. The monk doesn't speak English but I manage to convey fires. Australia. Now. He looks shocked, and accepts my offerings of beer and butter with such earnest concern that finally I start to feel better.

While few Bhutanese pay much attention to what is happening outside their borders, they do follow what is written about them in international media. Most Nepalese newspapers are critical and Western ones adoring, seeing Bhutan through a golden haze of the mythical Shangri-La, a fictional place in James Hilton's 1933 novel *Lost Horizon*. Hilton's Shangri-La is a seductive, hidden land in the Himalayas where people don't age and the overall religion is to be kind. The Shangri-La myth now permeates much of what is written about Bhutan.

A small Nebraska newspaper, *The Grand Island Independent*, publishes a story that features comments from bank worker Ken Bruce, who has returned from a trekking holiday in Bhutan. He tells the paper, 'Almost the entire country is extremely poor and cut off from surrounding society, but much of it is by choice … Many Bhutanese know about modern conveniences such as washing machines and television but choose not to use them.'

The idea that anybody would choose to be isolated and extremely poor is laughable. Everyone in Thimphu has the chance to cringe at such patronising ignorance when *Bhutan Times* analyses Ken's comments in its editorial titled 'Coffee table Bhutan'.

> The tourist must have felt the urge to tell his readers that he has reached an unstained country and use his Bhutan narrative as a moral bed time story for those spoilt by consumerism. The attempt is to market and domesticate an exotic experience for Western consumption and present Bhutan as a unique and clean product; [or] a zealous tour guide, in his attempt to present the best of Bhutan, added a little spice. Not his mistake, because he just did his job of making his guest happy and gave him a feeling that he has reached the best place on earth.

I'm guessing both are true and I feel some sympathy for poor, well-meaning Ken. Bhutanese tour guides can spin some bizarre lines, sometimes to keep their visitors happy and at other times out of sheer mischief. Visitors to Bhutan can't wander around on their own, catching local buses and booking into hotels as they feel like it. They must pre-book everything. Most visitors jet in on a two-week trek and are taken around the country by their guides, sleeping in tents and spending just one night at a hotel in Thimphu before they fly home.

Or they travel in four-wheel drives between a series of new uber-luxury resorts dotted around the country. Often the guides are the only Bhutanese people tourists talk to.

The guides don't always know the answers to all the tourists' questions, and what they don't know, sometimes they make up. Or when it comes to happiness, they stretch the truth, just a little, to make everyone feel good. They see it as their job. In many ways we are all complicit in this. The Bhutanese want Bhutan to be that Shangri-La as much for themselves as for tourists. And the tourists want it to be that way. That's why they come.

Dr Nitasha Kaul, an academic from the University of Westminster in London, conducts an analysis of international stories about the country's transition to democracy and writes about her findings in *Kuensel*. She concludes that Bhutanese coverage of the country's elections was far superior to that of the international media, which was stuck on this clichéd image of Bhutan, not unlike what Ken described. She lists some typical elements that the stories would include: references to a hidden Shangri-La, the four Queen Mothers, an isolated kingdom, the late introduction of television and the internet, and, of course, Gross National Happiness.

I understand why all those international stories about Bhutan can't get past these aspects of the country. They *are* newsworthy. No other country has them. No one is artificially imposing news value onto those aspects of Bhutanese life.

In Bhutan they call it Shangri-La journalism, and I'm guilty of it. Like Ken from Nebraska, I've done my bit to perpetuate the myth. In *A Baby in a Backpack to Bhutan* I managed to get most of Dr Kaul's list into my first page. I had nothing negative to say about the country – not a word – and for good reason: I didn't find anything negative.

My first visit was before the arrival of democracy and independent newspapers. The only newspaper was *Kuensel* and Phuntsho's family didn't get it at home. I used to watch the BBS news in English each night with them. Mostly it was about the Fourth King, government business, and education, with the odd banking fraud and a bit about traditional life in the villages. The two newsreaders looked elegant and polished in their *kira* and *gho*. BBS didn't cover topics such as alcoholism, drugs or domestic violence. It wasn't until years later, sitting in *Bhutan Observer* news conferences, that I learned about them. The topics are now openly reported and part of public discussion, but not then, just six years ago.

But most of all, my rose-coloured glasses came from living with Phuntsho's family. It was through them that I learned about Gross National Happiness, the extraordinary qualities of the Fourth King and the esoteric nature of the country. They took me to meet the Oracle, a lynx-like woman of mystical powers. While Mal was off up a yak trail making the film, they cared for Kathryn and me with such kindness and generosity that I still feel humbled when I remember it years later. They showed me their Bhutan – deeply spiritual, highly ethical and undoubtedly exotic. Bhutan may not be Shangri-La, but four months in that household came pretty close.

As a journalist, Kinley Dorji recognises the news appeal of the Shangri-La myth and considers it mostly harmless, a junior version of GNH.

'I don't think Shangri-La is a big deal. I think as a concept it is a little outdated. It's been the lead in a few thousand stories. It sounds good, makes people pick up the story. It's sexy. It should not be romanticised to the extent that you forget it is a real country with real people. To an extent, that is happening. Some of it is just a sale to get the tourists. But the Bhutanese must not forget it. We should not fool ourselves.

'GNH is much more sound. It actually has an academic construction. It's all about responsibility and not letting materialism and desire take over.'

Kay Kirby Dorji, however, considers the Shangri-La myth to be unhelpful. She believes it is a sentimental delusion. 'People come here and gush about how perfect it is. It's a great place, but it is in no way perfect ... I've been here too long. Bhutanese are just like everybody else. They are happy if they have money and can buy things for a comfortable life. I can't say there is anything wrong with that ... But I think we shouldn't kid ourselves that we are Shangri-La. And I think that is a good thing about the growth of the media here because that has spurred coverage of the less Shangri-La parts of society. There is a lot more coverage of drug problems. There is still a lot of denial going on but there is a lot more openness than there used to be.'

One of the problems with the myth is that Bhutan doesn't want to become a living museum, no matter how much tourists may like it. It's a fine line between preserving culture and forcing it to stagnate. Finding that line is a constant topic of public discussion. Cultural preservation is one of the pillars of Gross National Happiness, so it crops up in every new policy.

An interesting moment of self-reflection comes when *Kuensel* publishes a story about the Monpa tribe, a small community living in remote mountains. They are considered the earliest inhabitants of the country with their own language, music, and clothing made from nettles. *Kuensel* laments that this small group of 261 Monpas, living in 41 households across three villages, 'have lost their culture and tradition to the winds of modernisation'.

Nyontemo, 75, remembers wearing nettle clothes as a child, until her uncle brought her soft clothes made of cotton and wool. 'Who would want to spend time weaving these rough clothes when there is so much choice in the market?'

But while the *Kuensel* journalist finds this sad, the Monpas themselves appear quite happy to lose their old ways. They would rather listen to *rigsar*, the modern Bhutanese music on the radio, than their old traditional songs. They prefer the money they earn working on farms to the poverty they endured from bamboo weaving. And who could blame them for liking soft clothes against their skin, instead of nettle fibre? I don't suppose the Dutch want to go back to clogs either.

Dzongsar Khyentse Rinpoche stirs up the discussion in an opinion piece in *Kuensel.*

> Of course, one of the core pillars of GNH is culture, which is obviously very important for the identity and sovereignty of a nation. But keeping a rich tradition and culture vibrant and alive does not mean pushing people to do exactly what their ancestors did 50 or 100 years ago. If we try to do that, we will not only ruin the creativity and critical intellect of the young by teaching them to mimic rather than create, but we won't even keep our culture alive or survive as a nation in the modern world.
>
> Resisting change might serve a supposed purpose of GNH by encouraging people to be happy with what they have. But unwisely insisting on the mimicking of old habits also stifles avant-garde activity and innovation, fails to value excellence, and ends up settling for mediocrity. And in the end, that approach undermines rather than enhances GNH by making our culture static rather than dynamic.

It is a provocative act for a spiritual leader to question GNH, and his piece prompts a wide-ranging discussion in the newspapers about the point of preserving culture.

In 1999, Bhutan became the last country to get television, and the world looked on with great interest. Many prophesied that it would destroy the culture – Bhutan would become homogenised or Americanised. Four years later, Britain's respected *Guardian* newspaper published a story that upset many Bhutanese, portraying the country as suffering a crime wave brought on by the arrival of television. Journalists Cathy Scott-Clark and Adrian Levy wrote:

> Bhutan's isolation has made the impact of television all the clearer, even if the government chooses to ignore it ... One third of girls now want to look more American (whiter skin, blond hair). A similar proportion have new approaches to relationships (boyfriends not husbands, sex not marriage). More than 35% of parents prefer to watch TV than talk to their children. Almost 50% of children watch for up to 12 hours a day.

In 2003, only 15,000 homes had subscribed to cable. It's not possible that half the country's children were watching up to 12 hours of television. In general, Bhutanese children attend school five days a week, sometimes six. If they live too remotely to get to a school, their families are unlikely to have electricity, much less a television.

Nor did television alert the Bhutanese to the startling possibility of casual sex. Sex with or without a long-term relationship has been going on in Bhutan for ... well, forever. The *Guardian* journalists were imposing a paradigm of Western morality onto a culture that has never seen the world so rigidly.

The writers presented as evidence of their crime wave a dozen or so recent incidents – including a man driving his in-laws off a cliff in a drunken rage, six bank employees jailed for fraud, and a girl doing sex work in the border town of Phuentsholing. They said that though no-one could be sure, there was a wealth of evidence that the 'impatient, selfish society promoted by television' was a critical factor in these crimes. 'The 700,000 inhabitants ... had never experienced serious law-breaking before.'

Long before television arrived, Bhutan had serious crime. The country has suffered a prime ministerial assassination, bombings, murders, rapes, embezzlement and high-level corruption. Needrup told me the story of Desi Chakpa Sangay, who in the 1850s was given a *gho* impregnated by his enemies with the smallpox virus. His painful, grisly death has become legend. Bhutan has never been the crime-free fairyland that Scott-Clark and Levy portrayed.

When the two *Guardian* reporters arrived in Bhutan, the society was in the midst of a fierce debate about television's influence and many were worried about what it would mean. *Kuensel* was publishing readers' letters, editorials and interviews with community leaders, warning of its corrupting influence.

But television, according to people inside the country at the time, had also brought benefits. The government surveyed Thimphu residents in 2002, and 90 per cent of teachers and parents said television was educational, helping to boost children's level of thinking and ideas, and increasing their enthusiasm for co-curricular activities. A media impact study, published a few months after the *Guardian* story, showed that about two-thirds of respondents believed television had a good impact on Bhutanese society. Only 8 per cent thought it had a negative impact.

To say television brought crime to Shangri-La overnight is simplistic and glib. The discussion in Bhutan is far more sophisticated.

For the Bhutanese, now able to read the international press online, seeing what is written about them is sometimes a shock. Pek reported in her 2003 media impact study:

> People with internet access are now reading about what the world has to say about Bhutan. We find increasingly that the views about Bhutan may not be true … The UK *Guardian*, for example, reported on how television has led the Bhutanese astray and unleashed a crime wave of fraud, violence and even murder in Bhutan. A young government employee said that after reading the article, he has learnt not to believe everything that the media covers.

It's hard to quantify the influence of the *Guardian* story. The article was syndicated worldwide (I read it in Australia's *Good Weekend*) and continues to be re-posted on blogs from South Africa to Iraq and inside Bhutan. In February 2013, almost a decade after it was first published, a Dutch man provided a link to the story via Twitter, ready for a new generation to be misinformed about Bhutan and the effects of television. Such is the nature of the modern, globalised media.

The story is referenced in academic journal articles from institutions such as Harvard and Rutgers, all accepting Scott-Clark and Levy's assertion that television brought serious crime to Bhutan.

I recognise its central idea repeated in a story that appears about the 2008 coronation in the UK *Telegraph*. William Langley describes Bhutan as a kingdom in decline thanks to television:

> He [the Fifth King] was in a hurry to get back and begin bouncing Bhutan into the 21st century. So, upon his return from Oxford, he quickly convinced his father to embark on a fast and furious programme of modernisation. And this is where the current problems began. The first event to shake the kingdom out of its millennial slumber was the arrival of television.

Not only does Langley accept the idea that television ruined Shangri-La, but he makes a further leap in saying it was the idea of the new young monarch, hell-bent on modernising the country. Langley ends his report:

> Few would suggest that Jigme is an unsuitable monarch, but his enthusiasm for change sits uneasily in this strange, remote land where traditional dress is compulsory and foreign languages banned. Even as they were clearing up after the party, a significant number of the new King's subjects would have been wondering whatever happened to Shangri-La.

Foreign languages banned? For decades *Kuensel* published editions in Dzongkha, English and Nepalese. Hindi is widely understood, thanks to decades of Bollywood movies at the cinema in Thimphu's main street. A small Tibetan population continues to speak Tibetan. As for the people being unhappy with their new King and wondering what happened to Shangri-La, I can only think that Langley attended a different coronation in a different country.

Bhutan as fallen Shangri-La, ruined by television, is just one of a bewildering array of narratives developed by the international media. Bhutan can represent a moral fable, an inspiring ideal, a wholesome past, a different future. It can appear as the antithesis of the modern Western experience. Some of these narratives have been created by the Bhutanese, but most reflect us more than them. In trying to explain Bhutan, too often we end up framing it in our own paradigms.

But as each sliver is committed to print, digitised, stored and disseminated, it adds to the collective – a mix of sentimental, patronising, misunderstood caricatures that probably mean well but don't do Bhutan justice. Bhutan is as flawed as any other country, dealing with issues of crime, alcoholism, domestic violence, youth unemployment, racial tensions and poverty. Its people share the human frailties of greed, ignorance, anger and desire.

It is a society only just emerging from the feudal age and trying to face the modern world in an intellectually and spiritually robust way. If we are to fully appreciate and learn from Bhutan, then we need to look beyond the clichés we have created.

13

Work Habits

One Saturday afternoon, I arrive home from work in tears of frustration. Mal and Kathryn have spent a glorious morning trekking to the top of the ridge behind Tashi Pelkhil village, picnicking on apples from the orchards along the way. I have spent it in the office, achieving exactly nothing.

Saturday work hours are 9 am to midday. I'm there on time to print handouts and prepare for a 9.30 writing workshop, but of the ten or so reporters meant to attend, just one turns up.

A meeting in Phuntsho's office scheduled for 11.30 isn't much better. For the first 20 minutes I'm the only one there. At 11.50 the management group starts dribbling in, and we finally get underway at 12.10 – which is about when I thought I would be driving over the bridge to Tashi Pelkhil and starting my weekend with my family. For the next hour and a half we discuss the same things we discussed last Saturday. It is like being buried alive. Slowly. Not everyone came to the last meeting so we must go over it all again. But in re-opening the discussion, decisions that we made last week are rescinded and reconsidered. The sun pours through the window, reminding me what a beautiful day it is outside, and I feel light-headed from hunger as we go around the circle again and again to express our views. The Bhutanese value consensus, so everyone in the room must be heard. It is harmonious and inclusive but can also be intensely irritating when you actually want to get things accomplished. And the jobs allocated at the last meeting – find out this information, talk to that government department – are still yet to be completed, except for mine. I'm the only one who reports back with an update on my little patch. And to my rising irritation, no-one is held accountable for what they haven't done.

I complain to Mal about all the time-wasting but am hesitant to broach it with Phuntsho. These are her meetings. She's the boss. While it is part of my job to advise management, as much as it is to train reporters, I'm not comfortable criticising her personal performance. Mal, however, says I need to find a way. I'm not doing anybody any favours by sitting through pointless meetings and then seething with resentment about them.

I worry about it all weekend, before bringing it up with Phuntsho on Monday. I feel very Bhutanese as I dance around the topic, avoiding saying anything directly. I can see from her face that she has no idea what I'm trying to say. Finally I just blurt it out. *The meetings are not productive. Nobody does what they are supposed to. I'm going insane.* She is immediately receptive. She doesn't think she is very good at running meetings, she says, taking the blame I have so carefully avoided apportioning. She asks how she can improve.

This is management without ego, and I think it is one of the reasons Phuntsho achieves so much. She keeps herself open to suggestions and is flexible, willing to change direction on the spot.

Together we establish new protocols for office meetings. The office manager will take notes, identifying who is to do what, and provide a copy to everyone first thing on Monday mornings. Anybody absent will be briefed on decisions made before the next meeting. Everyone will turn up on time. Everyone will be accountable for their own tasks. It's a start.

*

I spend a lot of time trying to understand Bhutanese sensibilities when it comes to work. I realised when I was working on the *Faces of Bhutan* magazine that I was worrying about it away from work. Would there be any stories? Would we meet the deadline? I had assumed responsibility for it and taken on all the associated worries, but no-one else seemed to – the Bhutanese editor who was supposed to work with me missed every single deadline. Mal sympathises with me. When making *Travellers & Magicians* he realised the contrast between how much he was worrying and how little the Bhutanese were.

The Bhutanese are fluid about most things. People often don't keep appointments, but may suddenly appear in the offices as the Thursday-evening deadline looms. I'm amazed at how welcoming Needrup is to unexpected visitors when he is behind deadline and trying to write his weekly editorial. Phuntsho is the same. A distant cousin from her village drops by just when she has an important appointment at a government ministry, but they have tea and biscuits and a relaxed chat. If she is agitated, she doesn't show it.

It takes me months of being told the head of a department is 'at the bank' before I realise that on Mondays he doesn't come to work before 11 am. Ever. None of his department finds this strange. It's certainly not a sacking offence. Everyone simply works around him.

The arts editor suddenly takes off. He gives no warning or phone call explaining how long he might be gone. He just doesn't turn up for days, and then weeks. On his return, two and a half weeks later, he explains he had to settle his younger brother at college in India. It's not an apology or even a justification. He just mentions in passing that that's where he's been. I'm the only one who finds it odd.

Another editor takes a week off to sort out his marriage problems. The week turns into a month, then three months, until gradually it becomes clear that he isn't coming back.

Bhutan Observer is already short-staffed. When senior editors disappear, the other editors take over. No fuss. No animosity. No-one passes judgment or gets annoyed. It seems to be a common thread in Bhutanese relationships.

This lack of work ethic is endemic, both in the office of *Bhutan Observer* and throughout Thimphu. There is little sense of obligation to do the job you are paid to do. The Bhutanese consider it a national trait and laugh about it. They call it BST – Bhutan Stretchable Time. Newspapers write about the 'laziness' of the Bhutanese. The public send letters to the editors, bemoaning poor service in government offices. Druk Air flights are about the only thing in Bhutan that keeps to schedule. Somehow Bhutanese pilots manage to set their alarms and get to work on time, every time. It's the rest of the country that struggles.

On one hand I applaud the status that work is given: it is reassuring to find a place in the world where family, spiritual pursuits and even fun take precedence over earning money. But I also see the burden it places on everybody else. The newspaper, like any business, runs on a chain of delivery. If a deadline is missed, the effects flow through the whole company. The newspapers are late off the printing press, and instead of starting deliveries late on Thursday night, *Bhutan Observer*'s drivers have to deliver them throughout the day on Friday. That means drivers and cars won't be available to take the advertising staff around the government offices for 'collections', where they pick up the money for advertisements that week. Without that money, Tenzin can't pay staff their monthly wages.

Collections also give advertising staff the opportunity to seek advertisements for the following week. Bhutanese etiquette means face-to-face visits are crucial for any kind of business, and Fridays are the best day for them. If the opportunity is lost, it doesn't come again.

Not going on sale on Friday morning is also detrimental because it means that efforts to make the newspaper a reading habit are disrupted. The bumper weekend edition of *Kuensel* comes out on Saturday, so *Bhutan Observer* only has Friday to be newsy. When the newspaper is late, circulation income always drops. The newspaper's reputation suffers.

After a particularly bad few months for the newspaper, Phuntsho and her husband sell some family land to cover wages. Seeing how modestly they live and their earnest aspirations, I feel cross at their staff. When they don't turn up and do their jobs, the repercussions affect everyone else. It's that Buddhist notion of interdependence at work.

Phuntsho recognises the problem, but has no success fixing it. The attitude to work is deeply cultural. It is a reflection of the best of Bhutanese priorities … and also the worst. Phuntsho and Needrup have high hopes for the newspaper but when staff don't show up, achieving their goals is impossible.

Getting the reporters to work back is no problem. Evenings in the office are quite a social affair. It's getting them in to start the day that is a challenge. Needrup publicly scolds late reporters in news conferences. He is grave, authoritative and impressive. Their reaction? They laugh. It's a very Bhutanese response, which I've seen countless times and can't explain. It doesn't mean disrespect or disregard. It's just the way Bhutanese react to disapproval.

Phuntsho trials a system whereby reporters have to sign themselves in and out at reception. If they are late or don't turn up, she docks their pay. But despite their best efforts, little changes.

It takes a lot to lose a job on *Bhutan Observer.* Bad behaviour is tolerated to a degree that would be unacceptable anywhere else I've ever worked. Phuntsho and Tenzin are loath to sack anybody. The Bhutanese cultural trait of politeness makes firing someone highly unpalatable.

Even theft is excused. When the man in charge of distribution is discovered to have been pocketing the money he collected on behalf of the newspaper, I feel betrayed on Phuntsho's behalf. I know how tough it is for her and Tenzin to get this newspaper business up and running and I don't like seeing people take advantage of them. She asks what a newspaper proprietor would do in the West. I tell her stealing is one of the worst things an employee could do – they might be escorted from the building and required to pay back what they stole. Phuntsho looks horrified. There is no way she would inflict such humiliation on anyone.

For many months I marvel at the appalling behaviour of two staff members. One is lazy, not doing his job; the other is arrogant and rude to everyone around him. I would have pushed them out the door in disgust long ago, and probably given in to the desire for a short lecture about their character deficiencies along the way. Phuntsho and Tenzin see it differently. They accommodate the bad behaviour and when finally the parting of the ways does come, it is mutual. At first, I think this approach is too soft, but then I start to see its advantages. There is no ill feeling. Egos are left intact. No one loses face. In a small society, this means everything. Both the staff members leave with goodwill for the newspaper and its owners. There aren't enough capable writers in Bhutan, and within months both are contributing freelance stories to *Bhutan Observer.*

The cavalier approach to jobs seems odd in a country with no unemployment benefits. Everyone needs an income to live. I struggle to make sense of their attitude. On one hand they seem excessively subordinate to authority, but on the other hand they have little fear of losing their jobs.

Mystified, I talk to Kay Kirby Dorji. She explains that the extended family provides protection and, as a result, Bhutanese take longer to become independent. The lack of work ethic, she says, is a result of their 'extended adolescence'. She believes it is holding Bhutan back.

'There is this incredibly extended adolescence where they stay at home till they are about 30 years old. Everybody lives with Mummy and Daddy. Nobody gets out and stands on their own two feet and becomes independent. You have all these people who are 26, 27, pushing 30, still living with their parents, with no prospect of a job unless one of their relatives happens to own something,' says Kay.

'It's frightening because they are not learning independence, which I think is necessary for success. They are not being encouraged or pressured to get out there and take responsibility, be independent, become a productive member of society. It would be great if they could find a Buddhist middle path out of this, where they could keep the extended family ties but at the same time develop their own independence and self-worth. I think they are at one end of the spectrum, the West is at the other end, and the best path is the middle path.'

I feel torn. On the one hand I'm inspired that they are more interested in their families and spiritual pursuits than making money. But it also feels dishonest. Every business is interdependent. Every workplace relies on everyone doing their bit. This is not a case of exploited workers and the wealthy owners making all the money, and I feel disappointed when I see employees letting down Phuntsho and Tenzin.

I also feel a new appreciation for the work ethic that we espouse in the West, the expectation that you do the job you're paid for – or get sacked. As an employee you are accountable for your actions, and there is an honesty and integrity about that which I find appealing.

14

A Victory for the Media

Bhutan Observer's four rural reporters come to Thimphu for a week of writing workshops. I've been looking forward to meeting them, particularly Gyembo Namgyal, who lives in Pemagatshel, four days' travel away in the far east of the country. Gyembo is a legend. He did not finish school but I am told he reads books, lots of them. In a country that doesn't read, this is considered remarkable. Gyembo writes at least one feature each week, usually two or three. He ferrets out the most interesting characters and wonderfully bizarre stories in the south-east. When I read his features, I usually find myself smiling.

A month or so ago, management decided to offer Gyembo a job in head office. The paper was short-staffed, and giving him a promotion seemed a good solution. But when Tenzin personally phoned Gyembo to tell him of this news, Gyembo resigned on the spot. He didn't want to come to Thimphu.

Tenzin tried everything – cajoling, threatening, offering a pay rise and a more important job title. Nothing worked. Finally, after weeks of fruitless negotiations, he got to the root of the problem. Gyembo did not want to leave his cow. Tenzin suggested he bring it with him, saying there were plenty of cows in Thimphu. But Gyembo felt his cow was too old to travel such a long distance. Perhaps when the cow died he might reconsider, but for now he wanted to stay in Pemagatshel. And so he did.

Gyembo arrives two days late thanks to a landslide on the main highway that delayed his bus. He is a fascinating mix of the modern and the uniquely Bhutanese. Like all the reporters, he's on Facebook, but his world revolves around his cow. He is tall and solid, with a gentle manner and a colourful, beautifully pressed *gho.* I like him immediately.

I also meet Tempa Wangdi, from Trashigang, slightly north of Gyembo's region. He is Gyembo's opposite in every way. I am only 168 centimetres tall, and he barely reaches my shoulder. He is a frenetic ball of energy, with darting eyes, and is irrepressibly cheeky. It is impossible not to like him, though I imagine he would be exhausting to live with. I discover that although he is happily married, his wife lives elsewhere. He is extremely pleased to be called to the head office – not to do my writing workshops, he tells me cheerfully, but because he has a few issues to sort out with management. He would like a filing cabinet and a motorbike. Also, an increase in travel allowances. Horse porters in his region have raised their rates, so the cost of getting around the villages and yak camps and mountaintop monasteries has also risen. These issues are being ignored and it is time management addresses them, he tells me within minutes of walking in the door. He is like a small, highly charged rocket.

We end up with the four rural reporters, five Thimphu reporters and two staff from Bhutan's media regulatory authority, BICMA. In a country with such little media experience, Phuntsho thinks my workshops are an opportunity for them to learn too. So does their boss, the head of BICMA, who also has no media experience but is too important to attend himself.

While the reporters are a confident bunch, used to each other and keen to talk about writing, the two BICMA staff are clearly terrified.

They sit hunched together, avoid eye contact with anyone else, and don't join in discussions. On the second day, they don't even turn up.

We hold the workshops in the boardroom, where I stand at the whiteboard as a woman waves to me from the roof next door. She is placing small stick figures made from twigs and rags to scare away evil deities. Smoke is swirling about her. It is an odd sight. The sound of monks chanting rolls in through the windows.

Our workshop agenda includes grammar, editing, writing headlines, writing news and writing features. The Thimphu reporters come and go according to the stories they need to cover. The rural reporters stay for it all, soaking up everything. They are enthusiastic and fun. Each session ends up wildly off topic.

Tempa asks what I think about reading. He says he read about a man who is psychic and can see into people's pasts and futures. What do I think of that?

I say I don't know.

But it is in a book!

I reply that people can make things up in a book just like they can in conversation. He looks shocked. Gyembo, the reading legend, says he was told not to read fiction, that it is 'dangerous' for journalists. I tell him I don't think that is true, and he looks relieved.

In the middle of a session Tempa takes a call on his mobile phone. Bhutanese never turn off their phones in meetings, so we all get to enjoy the discussion. One of the reporters translates for my benefit. It is a reader, angry that in a story Tempa called his village a ghost town.

'We don't have ghosts,' the reader shouts at Tempa through the phone.

Tempa explains that the phrase 'ghost town' means 'empty of people, deserted'. The village was relocated, everyone moved out, and now it was just a deserted collection of buildings. A ghost town.

The man has no idea what Tempa is talking about. 'Why won't you admit you made a mistake and write an apology?' he yells.

Tempa argues, 'But I didn't.'

The man swears at him and hangs up.

Tempa grins. Criticism from readers, or anybody else, rolls off his back. This is fortunate, as it seems it is his karma to upset people. During the workshops, he writes a story for the newspaper about his three-day bus journey coming to Thimphu. It is an exposé on the bus driver who brought him here. He writes that the driver took on more passengers than was allowed, overcharged many of the passengers for their tickets and charged extra for luggage. Furthermore, the driver refused to stop the bus for a child to go to the toilet, so she wet herself, but he did stop the bus to flirt with some pretty young women. He also stopped for breakfast at 9 am, and then lunch at 10 am. From what I understand, the bus driver's actions are not unusual, but it is the first time such behaviour has been detailed in a newspaper. Tempa's story sets in motion a chain of events.

In a country of rickety old buses and vertiginous mountain passes, being overloaded can be catastrophic. Accidents on the national highway are part of the collective psyche in the same way bushfires and shark attacks are part of the Australian psyche. But it goes much, much deeper. The national highway is the spine of Bhutan – literally and figuratively. It runs from east to west, cutting through mountain passes at altitudes ranging from 3,500 to 4,000 metres above sea level.

Engineering feat aside, what makes the road truly remarkable and the pride of the country is that the people built it, inch by inch, breaking up the rocks by hand. They were not paid. They just responded to the call of the Third King, coming from the villages and farms to donate their time and labour. It is how the Bhutanese build *lhakhangs* and schools, and clear communal land. They have a name for it: *Druk dom woola*. There is no English translation. Or equivalent practice.

The national highway was started in May 1961 and finished in 1988. Given the dense forests and sheer rock faces, it is hardly surprising it took 17 months to build the first nine kilometres of road. According to an engineer who oversaw the first year of building, every Bhutanese man, woman and child in the area worked for 33 days building the first stretch of road. The government brought in Indian engineers and mechanics, but it was the Bhutanese who did the hard slog.

In the book by Tim Fischer and Tshering Tashi, *Bold Bhutan Beckons*, Australian engineer Hardy Pradhan said that what amazed him most was how happy the people were at work. Tshering writes: 'They were proud to be participating in the building of a modern nation and worked hard simply because their King had asked them to do so. Hardy also said that it was difficult for him to explain to Westerners this concept of affection and loyalty to a monarch.'

When the first few kilometres of road were completed, the Third King wanted to try it out. A jeep was dismantled, all its parts transported by mule along narrow passes and over high trails, then reassembled for him to drive from one end to the other. The Queen Mother wrote that the local people thought the jeep was a fire-breathing dragon, with its blazing headlights and roaring engine.

The Third King originally expected that one in six people would volunteer, but by the time the road was finished, 27 years later, one in every three Bhutanese had laboured on that road. It was dirty, back-breaking, dangerous work that included digging, blasting and, for some, dangling precariously over cliff edges on ropes to place explosives. In the warmer southern regions, there were malarial mosquitoes. Elsewhere, heavy rains and the unstable mountains produced frequent landslides. All in all, 700 people lost their lives.

Despite the hardships, Hardy remembered the singing and the laughter of the workers. He described toddlers playing while women broke up rocks and gossiped. Working alongside the Bhutanese were Tibetan refugees who had fled the Chinese military invading their country. Hardy said they were relieved to be in a Buddhist country where they were showered with affection. There were also Nepalese workers who lived inside the border. The construction was a great social leveller in this feudal country.

In 1974, Bhutan celebrated the coronation of the Fourth King. The fleet of Ford Falcons that Australia gave Bhutan to mark this auspicious occasion were to be driven on the section of road that had been finished. They became their own legend, the first cars in the country. A new Rolls-Royce ferried the Indian president while the Ford Falcons followed in a majestic procession, each one carrying a dignitary or an ambassador. The people who lined the road were awestruck by the sight of all those cars, not knowing whether to bow or flee.

Mal remembers being driven in the last surviving Falcon when he first visited Bhutan in the early nineties. Over the years it had been repaired using bits and pieces from all the others.

Our friend Sonam says that although he was just five, he vividly remembers the shiny metal beasts passing by. He had never seen anything so grand or mysterious in his life. These days, as a successful civil servant in his forties, with a PhD from Cornell University in America, he gets around the traffic of Thimphu in his own Toyota Prado.

According to Tshering Tashi, the national highway changed everything. Basic necessities such as salt and sugar became available and affordable to ordinary people. Farmers could get their produce to markets. It was possible to develop infrastructure in more corners of the country. Bhutan launched itself from medieval ways into the 20th century, at last realising the Third King's vision.

The highway connects east and west, but entire regions still are long distances from a major road. It is faster to get from America to Thimphu, changing planes along the way, than it is to drive from eastern Bhutan to the capital. The Bhutanese describe distances in terms of days' travel rather than kilometres. They are happy to walk for days – hundreds of kilometres – to visit family or attend a *tshechu*. The Fifth King does it regularly to keep in touch with his people.

The national highway is important to Bhutan in both symbolic and practical terms. Landslides that block great swathes of road can delay the supply of food to Thimphu market, rob farmers of income, and delay the Fifth King en route to visiting a town. Car accidents on the hairpin bends or over the steep cliffs are tragically common. The highway occupies a unique place in Bhutanese life and is a constant source of news.

When *Bhutan Observer* publishes Tempa's story about the negligent bus driver, it provokes a storm. The driver is sacked, and for a while Tempa becomes known as the reporter who exposed the bus driver.

The driver asks *Bhutan Observer* to issue a retraction. Phuntsho refuses. The story is true and they were right to publish it, she says. So the driver sues for defamation, one of the new democracy's first such cases.

The trial lasts a week and is reported on by all the newspapers. Other passengers testify that the bus was overloaded. The driver is caught out lying, and he changes his story. As the trial unfolds, he starts to look more dishonest. Unable to bear the man's public humiliation, an official court representative takes Phuntsho aside and asks if she could just publish an apology and pay him some money. Let him save face. Had the driver not suffered enough?

Phuntsho is indignant.

'No. We are a newspaper. We tell the truth,' she tells him. 'It's important. That's what we do.'

The court representative argues that it would be simpler – and kinder – if *Bhutan Observer* did what it could to restore harmony.

'But we're a newspaper. We can't say we were wrong when we weren't,' she replies.

Phuntsho is quite clear on the role of the media in this new democracy. It is about truth, which is important for the community. She becomes frustrated that the court official doesn't see that.

She tries to explain that the newspaper's credibility would suffer. It has to tell the truth, as best it can.

Phuntsho represents the modern face of Bhutan. Democracy may not always be kind, but it aims to be fair. The court official is not convinced: he sees things the old way. Saving face and showing compassion are more important.

Because Phuntsho will not budge, the case is returned to court. The judge finds that Tempa's story was true and rules in favour of *Bhutan Observer.*

It is a victory for the media.

15

Wooden Phalluses and Crooked Vaginas

Like all Bhutanese government offices and businesses, *Bhutan Observer* has a box of condoms mounted on the wall at reception. The government supplies them to help fight AIDS. Every time I look the box is empty, which I'm told is typical. Offices throughout Thimphu have trouble keeping up with demand. The government supplies condoms in a range of colours, some with feathers and ribbing.

When it comes to sex, the Bhutanese go about it in their own unique way – as the ritual of night-hunting shows. Sometimes they can seem very relaxed, often ribald, while at other times downright prim. Everyone dresses demurely, and even in summer, flesh remains hidden. Siok Sian Pek-Dorji's media impact study shows how uncomfortable Bhutanese people feel at overtly sexual scenes on foreign television channels. A Thimphu mother said: 'It is not right to show underpants and breasts in public.' Others thought it was fine for *chillips* to be nude on television, but Bhutanese people should keep themselves covered up. City people thought it was inappropriate for families in the villages to be confronted by images of scantily dressed foreigners.

But that doesn't mean sex is taboo in Bhutan. One of the country's national heroes is a spiritual master from the 15th century, Drukpa

Kinley. Known as the Divine Madman, he exposed hypocrisy and pretentiousness wherever he found it, skewering our tendencies towards self-reverence. He wandered around with a staff shaped like a penis, was often naked, and became renowned as a master of tantra, using sex to help his consorts attain a state of transcendent bliss. He sang bawdy songs and used desire, emotion and sexuality to make his points.

Dr Sonam Kinga, founding editor-in-chief of *Bhutan Observer* and renowned scholar, wrote in a paper: 'Drukpa Kinley used the phallus as a medium to tame the demons and demonesses and other malevolent spirits, and in his sexual practices to overcome the social inhibitions set by the socially established values.'

While his methods often appeared shocking, to the Bhutanese he manifested a particular form of enlightenment known as 'crazy wisdom'. He is considered a saint.

Bhutanese children grow up hearing outrageous stories about the Divine Madman and quietly absorb the key point of these tales, which is Drukpa Kinley's irreverence for rigid moral codes. Despite the highly structured social hierarchy in Bhutan, there is also a certain respect for unconventionality that runs through the culture, as well as an openness about sexuality.

While publicising *Travellers & Magicians* in 2004, Dzongsar Khyentse Rinpoche told American journalist Noa Jones:

> While the Bhutanese live by values which agree, on the most part, with universal systems and morals, there is also a unique set of values, particular to Bhutan, that is unlike anything found in other Asian countries. For example, in many parts of Bhutan the subject of sex is not so taboo as it is in China, India or Tibet ... Other cultures have lost this sense of freedom or openness, in turn possibly making them into sexually repressed societies. So-called sophistication may have made their minds narrow and rigid, depriving them of a source of happiness.

This goes some way towards explaining the Bhutanese bawdy humour. Phuntsho comes back from a week of teachings with Dzongsar Khysentse Rinpoche in eastern Bhutan and I find her in her office still giggling from some of the Bhutanese jokes. Rinpoche was collecting them and asked all the Bhutanese to volunteer their best. Phuntsho tells me her favourite.

'The dog says to the rooster, "Don't stand near me, you are an embarrassment. You have a clitoris on your head and testicles hanging from your ears." The rooster says, "When you sit down your balls are in the dirt."'

She convulses into another round of giggles. I smile politely but finally confess I don't find it rip-roaringly funny. This sends her off again into peals of laughter. When she can compose herself, she tells me Westerners were present at the teachings, but even when the jokes were translated into English, they did not understand them, looking confused as the Bhutanese fell about in hysterics. Phuntsho finds this the funniest thing of all.

While Tibetans also revere Drukpa Kinley for his crazy wisdom and sexual openness, the Bhutanese are on their own in the way they celebrate the phallus. Erect penises are on display everywhere. Paintings of penises and testicles adorn houses, and the images are not subtle. Some have curly black hair around the shaft, even froth coming out of the tip. Creative rural people sculpt the phallic form into useful things like satellite dish holders and fountains. To the Bhutanese, there is nothing lewd about publicly displaying the phallus.

I'm told that the simple explanation, which tour guides pass on to tourists, is that phallic symbols ward off evil spirits, protect against the evil eye or increase fertility. A more complex explanation is that the phallus, representing the human body and its inherent wisdom, is an antidote to the evil of materialism and the suffering caused by attachment.

People hang a wooden phallus from the eaves on the four corners of their home. They 'cross' the shaft through the centre with a sword. The phallus and the sword represent opposite impulses – the phallus is earthly desire, or ego, and the sword represents wisdom. Together they negate each other, leading to the symbolic taming of the human mind.

In central Bhutan, hosts are likely to dip a wooden phallus in your tea before serving it to you. At the *tshechus*, a man dressed like a crazy court jester weaves through the crowds while waving a vivid red phallus and poking it suggestively at everyone – old women, monks, nuns, children, parliamentarians. The audience falls about laughing. It is not rude or sexual. It is irreverent and very, very funny. Everyone is in on the joke.

At a news conference, reporter Rabi talks about a remote town where the women have unique anatomy. After entertaining everybody with the ribald details, he decides he really should investigate the story and disappears for a week. He returns with a story for the features pages.

Crooked female genitalia and the legend that straightened things out

Phu is crooked and so are vaginas, say the men of a remote village in Lhuentse. Rabi C. Dahal explores this quaint little story.

Some distance above Ungar village in Metso Gewog in Lhuentse is a curiously tilted ridge, which the locals say houses and represents the village's guardian deity, Phushing Liphung Tsangpo. The ridge lists to the right, supposedly the result of a right-handed slap on the deity's face by her husband, Numgmabri.

The legend goes that, one day, Phushing refused to entertain Numgmabri as she was busy weaving. Numgmabri got annoyed and tried to steal the weaving thread and run away but Phushing was quick enough to stop him by hitting him with the tam (weaving beater), resulting in a deep cut to the head. Numgmabri responded by slapping her so hard her face became tilted.

It is said that Numgmabri and Phushing parted ways thereafter. He settled down in Tongebi-Galiping village in the same gewog while she stopped weaving altogether. To this day, her remorse continues to be borne by the women in Ungar. None of them weave.

Like all the men in the village, Ugyen Tenzin, 63, believes their women bear the after-effects of Phushing and Numgmabri's fight in another way. 'The elders used to tell us that the vagina is crooked because Phushing is crooked,' he said.

The women, though, beg to differ. They said the men's belief is a fallacy. Phushing may be crooked but the vagina is straight.

16

New Ideas

In my daily meetings with Phuntsho, we come up with lots of ideas for the company. It is exhilarating. She is always thinking of the children, Bhutan's next generation, and how to help them. As levels of education improve, the need for books will increase. She suggests a range of children's books telling Bhutanese folk tales. The elders pass on these tales orally, and it would just be a matter of collecting them. Perhaps we could also translate into Dzongkha the Jataka tales, stories of the Buddha's pre-incarnations before he gained enlightenment.

The lifestyle pages of the newspaper have started publishing favourite family recipes, the ones passed down from *ama* to *ama*. We could publish an annual cookbook, preserving Bhutanese traditions while appealing to tourists.

The company already distributes newspapers across the country, so perhaps we could try book distribution? A book club? A weekly lift-out television guide? There is a never-ending conversation about finding new channels of revenue using the company's limited resources.

Tenzin, who is knowledgeable about all things to do with printing, looks into the idea of security printing. The arrival of sophisticated photocopy machines has opened new opportunities for fraud, and

Bhutan sends its sensitive printing – such as lottery tickets, exam papers and share certificates – to India or Thailand. It's a great idea, and Tenzin applies for funding from a Danish aid agency for purpose-built presses. His vision also includes facilities for the disabled. In 2004, he visited Kentucky as part of a Bhutanese delegation and was profoundly moved to see disabled people at a printing press, working alongside able-bodied people. Blind people operated machines, doing folding, collating, inserting, counting and whatever else was required. He would like to provide employment for disabled people in Bhutan.

I find a Japanese–English magazine on the internet that looks interesting. It publishes one paragraph of a story in Japanese, immediately followed by the same paragraph in English. Phuntsho and Tenzin are always trying to offset the costs of the Dzongkha edition, which attracts no advertising but requires translators, an editor, and all the costs of printing and distribution. Each week the best stories in *Bhutan Observer* are translated into Dzongkha. This means every week the newspaper produces a mirror copy of stories, so a bilingual edition could be a new stream of income at little extra cost. We talk about the feasibility of a small monthly paper with a selection of features, presented in the two languages side by side. It would be helpful to anyone trying to learn the other language. It could be a wonderful resource for schoolchildren, civil servants and parliamentarians. Dzongkha is the language of government, and those who don't speak it well are disadvantaged. The Dzongkha Development Commission, responsible for promoting the language, might consider sponsoring it. It could sell for the same cost as the newspaper, or a little more.

I show the Japanese–English magazine to Phuntsho, and she asks me to present the idea at the next management meeting. The response is not quite of the level of enthusiasm I was expecting. The editors are wary. We discuss it again at the next management meeting and I think I detect a mild stirring of interest. We discuss names, and I suggest

Double Feature, Two Worlds, The Monthly. No one says directly that they hate them, but it is clear they do. I feel gauche. They want something more … Dzongkha-like.

The Dzongkha edition of *Bhutan Observer* is called *Druk Nelug*, which they explain means 'as it is'. It is not a direct translation because it is not possible to give one. *Druk Nelug* encompasses all sorts of nuances that the English language cannot accommodate. They throw around possible Dzongkha titles. *Rigphel* looks like a winner for a moment, then one of the editors suggests *Lophel*. They all consider the word, repeating it again and again before deciding that they like it. They tell me that, once again, there is no English equivalent but it conveys a sense of gravitas. They find it evocative: even the word itself sounds beautiful. It means 'wisdom', but in a special way. They may as well be explaining a colour I've never seen, but at least they have chosen a name that means something to them, which I think means they are coming around to the idea.

Later, Phuntsho asks me if I like the name. She is clearly pleased with it. It is rich with layers of meaning for her, truly lovely in some way I fail to appreciate. To me the word means nothing and even sounds a little clumsy. I confess to her that I'm not a big fan but only because I don't appreciate the nuances of the word and Dzongkha sounds are foreign to me, but I assure her I am pleased that everyone else is excited about it. She looks disappointed and I feel gauche again. We have a different verbal aesthetic, I offer lamely. I ponder it for days afterwards and find myself wondering what English sounds like to the Bhutanese ear. Bland? Lazy? What does it sound like to Germans? Italians? I try but simply am unable to will myself into the mindset of another culture.

We discuss *Lophel* at the next three management meetings but don't get anywhere. Each week we talk ourselves into it and out of it again. The features editor says that if the Dzongkha Development Commission advertises in the publication, we can't ask people to pay for it. This mystifies me. But people buy *Bhutan Observer* and that has government advertisements, I explain. That is the business model for the newspaper. He looks unconvinced.

The following week he says he thinks it would be detrimental for the newspaper's image if we brought out something that was no good, so perhaps it would be best not to do it. It's paralysis by analysis. I feel my frustration rise: it shouldn't be this hard, but it is. I can't put my finger on why there is such reluctance. It seems everything to do with Dzongkha is complex. The scholars cannot agree on words and keep changing the rules. Phuntsho says a lot of what she learned at school has now been changed. But there is more to it, something about the status of the language that I am not grasping, a subtle snobbery or respect for Dzongkha that goes beyond how I view my own language. They view Dzongkha as being inherently sacred. The script, which is related to Tibetan, is elegant and drawn in fluid strokes. But their reverence goes beyond its physical form. The Buddhist masters talk about language and letters in profoundly spiritual terms. Not all of the management team are devout Buddhists, but those teachings are in the air they have been breathing since birth. They share a feeling for Dzongkha that is outside my experience.

Despite their reservations, we agree to proceed with a trial edition. Two editors collect features for the next four weeks and Sushil lays it out. He designs a glossy brown cover with an orange title *Lophel* in English and Dzongkha. It is printed in Thimphu on A6 pages, small enough to roll up and carry in the front of a *gho* or *kira* or in a handbag. I think it looks pretty good.

Lophel is a failure. The first and only edition is riddled with errors. I can't see them myself, because they are in the Dzongkha sections. In our next management meeting we discuss why. It soon becomes apparent that whoever was supposed to proofread it failed to do so, but we skirt around this obvious fact. It may be a cultural reaction: to lay blame on a senior member of staff in front of the others might involve too much loss of face. Or it may be something else, something about what Dzongkha means to this society. Certainly no-one seems to share my disappointment that it did not work. The team is unanimous that we should not produce another issue and that is the end of that.

Mentally I file it away among the things I will never understand and we move on. Tenzin is printing calendars, featuring *Bhutan Observer* cartoons, for advertisers. Phuntsho wants to hold an education conclave to improve our schools page. And the advertising department has suggested a distribution drive getting taxi drivers to sell copies of *Bhutan Observer* to their passengers. There is lots to do.

Phuntsho decides we should start working on a second edition of *Faces of Bhutan*. The media impact study of 2008 showed that Bhutanese want to read about what's happening in their own country, and see their own faces and traditions reflected in their media, so we decide this edition should be about Buddhism in Bhutan. There are some extraordinary masters here who draw huge crowds when they travel to the West to give teachings. There are also sacred sites of great power and relevance. The magazine could have a story about the mad, phallus-waving Drukpa Kinley, master of crazy wisdom. As well as being a Bhutanese hero, he is an object of fascination for any practitioner of Vajrayana Buddhism, as his life and teachings demonstrated a mind free from constraints.

We could feature Yeshe, an example of the thousands who are undertaking private retreats in caves and mountaintops across the country. A *lhakhang* above Thimphu has deep grooves in the wooden floor, which have been gouged there over the past decade by a monk doing daily prostrations. They are a hauntingly beautiful sight. Bhutan has a wealth of such stories.

As well as showing Bhutan its own remarkable spiritual heritage, we expect this edition to appeal to Western Buddhists. Three Buddhist magazines are published in America: *Tricycle*, *Buddhadharma* and *Shambhala Sun*. They carry advertisements for books, retreats, tours and teachings of various Buddhist masters. We would hope to capture the same international readership and target some of their advertisers.

Given that distribution inside Bhutan is always a challenge, getting copies to America sounds almost insane. But Mal suggests that a digital edition might work. Since we moved to Bhutan, he has received his monthly *Mac/Life* magazine as a digital download. He loves it and says he doesn't want to go back to print. I investigate this possibility and discover Zinio on the internet: it is a digital magazine company that does just what we need.

The newspaper staff contribute stories, and Dzongsar Khyentse Rinpoche agrees to let us publish a chapter from his new book, *What Makes You Not a Buddhist*. A Welsh monk, Lama Shenpen, works with troubled youth in Thimphu and is a good friend of Phuntsho and Tenzin. He proposes an article on ethics for a Buddhist media. 'In countries that preserve Buddhist wisdom, understanding of interdependence should form the core of news reporting,' he writes.

Karma Ura, an Oxford alumnus and perhaps Bhutan's foremost intellectual, writes about the distinctly Bhutanese flavour of Vajrayana Buddhism and the spiritual meaning of the phalluses. He argues that Western media flaunts the female body on billboards, while in Bhutan it is the opposite. The phalluses drawn on walls instead 'collapse' male sexuality. I find myself still thinking about his words days later.

Professor Bob Thurman, an expert on Bhutan and Vajrayana Buddhism from Columbia University, has just left Thimphu after giving a public talk. Now back in New York, he agrees to an interview over the phone about Buddhism in Bhutan and whether a Western form is evolving. It is a prickly subject in the Buddhist world: the cultural trappings of Buddhism can make it inaccessible to Westerners, who can baulk at the sight of a shrine or the concept of a guru. But separating the essence of Buddhism, the universal teachings of the Buddha, from the cultural aspects can be fraught. Professor Thurman has lots of interesting things to say.

I find my way to an exiled Tibetan lama, Mynak Tulku Rinpoche, who is great friends with the Queen Grandmother. Over tea in his apartment, I ask whether he would write about the very special relationship between the Queen Grandmother and the late great master Dilgo Khyentse Rinpoche. Her Majesty is a spiritual inspiration to the Bhutanese. They adore her. Dilgo Khyentse, who was the Dalai Lama's principal teacher, was a spiritual giant. The Queen Grandmother and the Third King gave him safe haven when he fled Tibet. She was both his royal patron and devout student. Mynak Tulku Rinpoche says he will ask.

The Queen Grandmother not only says yes to being interviewed, but also gives us photos from her private album. She believes it will benefit others to know about the life of the great Dilgo Khyentse Rinpoche.

On the internet I discover that the award-winning American photographer Mimi Kuo-Deemer has just completed a photo essay on the nuns of Bhutan for a UN project. I email her a request to use her photographs – once again explaining we have no money to pay for the images. Nevertheless, she sends me back ten stunning portraits of nuns, aged seven to 75, each with a short story about their lives. The faces are compelling, looking straight down the lens. Nuns throughout the Buddhist world are treated rather shabbily. They are considered lucky if they get to serve the monks tea during a teaching, and they get a fraction of the monks' funding and resources. To choose that life, and then dedicate yourself to it, takes a remarkable human being. Their stories are both heartbreaking and heartwarming.

The chief photographer for Reuters in India, Desmond Boylan, photographed the coronation of the Fifth King and puts all his photos at the disposal of *Bhutan Observer*. We can use them in this magazine or any other that the newspaper chooses to produce in future. This is truly astounding behaviour in the publishing world.

The ancient monastery of Taktshang (Tiger's Nest) was built over a cave where Guru Rinpoche meditated in the eighth century. It is Bhutan's most iconic landmark.

Right: Mal and Kathryn among the clouds at beautiful Dochula Pass, where the Queen Grandmother built 108 *chortens*, or Buddhist shrines, as an offering.

Below: Kathryn and her classmates wear their very best *kiras* and *ghos* for the Sunshine School end-of-year concert.

Tenzin Wangdi and Phuntsho Wangmo, owners of *Bhutan Observer.*

BHUTAN OBSERVER

The Independent Voice

Vol. III, Issue 41 FRIDAY OCTOBER 17 2008 Nu 10

The coronation begins

Briefly

Rats in the rice

The gift rule

DPT coordinator changed the road plan?

BHUTAN OBSERVER VACANCY

BAFRA

Bhutan Observer's front page on 17 October 2008.
(Courtesy of *Bhutan Observer*)

The *Bhutan Observer* staff outside their office building. *Clockwise from top left:* political cartoonist Chimi Namgyal (CN); head of advertising Gopal Singh (GS); graphic designer Sushil Mishra (SM); editor-in-chief Needrup Zangpo (NZ); senior reporter Rabi Dahal (RD); senior reporter Tandin Pem (TP).

A crowd gathers in the courtyard of Tashichhodzong during the celebrations for the Fifth King's coronation on 1 November 2008.
(Courtesy of Desmond Boylan)

The Fourth King places the crown on the Fifth King's head.
(Courtesy of *Bhutan Observer*)

The Fourth King's four wives celebrate the coronation.
(Courtesy of Desmond Boylan)

A ewe with an extra horn coming out of his nose is considered an auspicious gift for a King.

Two boy monks at their monastery in Bumthang. Nearly 10 per cent of the Bhutanese population are monks and nuns.

Prayer flags near Trongsa Dzong, the former seat of government and a major monastic complex in the centre of Bhutan.

Left: Yeshe and his kitten outside his temple, just before he begins his three-year retreat.

Below: A guest house in Phobjikha is decorated with traditional paintings, including a phallus.

Rita washes clothes in the drain outside the toilet block where she lives with her family.

I'm next to Dasho Neten Zangmo, the head of the Anti-Corruption Commission and the most powerful woman in Bhutan.

Tim Fischer, who has been instrumental in building bonds between Australia and Bhutan, stands with historian Tshering Tashi in front of a rock painting of Guru Rinpoche.

Prime Minister Tshering Tobgay, pictured here in 2011 when he was Opposition leader, has been a digital media pioneer in Bhutan. He started one of the country's first blogs, and led the way on Twitter and Facebook.

These massive embroidered *thongdrels* show sacred figures such as Guru Rinpoche and Buddha, and are unfurled for special occasions. This photo was taken in the courtyard at Tashichhodzong; I'm in the bottom right corner.

While browsing online I find some rare early photographs of Taktshang, Bhutan's most sacred site, before the great fire of 1998 that almost destroyed the original buildings. Taktshang, or Tiger's Nest, is an ancient monastery that clings to a cliff face 900 metres above the floor of the Paro valley. It is said that Guru Rinpoche, who took Buddhism from India to Tibet, flew here in 747 AD on the back of a tigress. He meditated for three months in a cave and concealed a teaching about spiritual materialism, to be discovered in the degenerate age, when it would be needed. The monastery was built over and around the cave. In 1968, a young Tibetan lama, Chogyam Trungpa Rinpoche, was passing through on his way to Europe and stayed at Taktshang, where he 'discovered' that teaching. When he came down from Taktshang, he had a vision for how he would spread Buddha's teachings in the West. He went on to found the Naropa University in Colorado, and established more than 100 meditation centres in America and Canada. He was often controversial and is considered another master of crazy wisdom.

Although he died in 1987, the website *Chronicles of Chogyam Trungpa Rinpoche* continues to publish his teachings, and it is there that I chance on a slideshow of his legendary visit to Taktshang. I email them asking if we can publish the photos in *Faces of Bhutan*. They send back three original photos and a story from a British student who was on that journey. His account of how Chogyam Trungpa Rinpoche revealed the ancient hidden teaching is riveting, and the photos of the sacred site, which is so much a part of the Bhutanese psyche, are bound to generate a lot of interest.

Despite these contributions, we still need more pictures for the magazine. Mal, Kathryn and I borrow a four-wheel drive and the office's new SLR camera, and head off for two weeks into the centre of Bhutan, taking photos as we go. Freewheeling around the country is not the way foreigners usually travel about Bhutan and the bigger hotels turn us away, suspicious of what we are doing in their midst.

We find beds in rustic family hotels, Kathryn often sleeping on a pile of cushions on the floor. They have no televisions, and sometimes no electricity, so each evening, by flickering firelight, Mal reads us a couple of chapters of the Harry Potter books before bed. The magic and spells that JK Rowling writes about seem entirely believable here, where locals tell of the demoness who lives in their valley, or the rock that holds their grandmother's spirit, or the zombie *rolongs* that haunt villages.

When we return to Thimphu, we hand over all our photos to Sushil, and he sprinkles them throughout the magazine. None of our pictures, however, seem strong enough for the front cover, so we go to Flickr, the place where tourists like to show off their images. Bhutan does not take a bad photo and there are dozens that could work. I send emails explaining my request for a cover image. Some people ignore me, one British man is offended I would even ask, but one person comes back with a yes. The photographer, Yeshey Dorji, is a Bhutanese tour guide turned professional photographer with a photo blog and six years' worth of glorious images. I had been told there was no such thing as a professional photographer in Bhutan and yet here he is, strutting his stuff on Flickr. I email him and he personally brings in his image of a gorgeous young monk smiling whimsically at the camera. He would be honoured if we used it for the cover. No need for payment.

While Sushil is laying out the magazine, Needrup comes into my office, grinning. He hands me an official-looking document with fancy seals, all written in Dzongkha. It looks impressive but I have no idea what it is. He explains it is from the Je Khenpo, the head of the monk body. He has written a foreword for the magazine. Needrup reads it out to me, translating as he goes:

> Today, because of materialistic and progressive development in science and economy in most parts of the world, people's minds

and thoughts are naturally diverging from the spiritual path. Consequently, it is common knowledge that as human society is increasingly afflicted by modern ills like conflicts, diseases, poverty, theft and murder, security, happiness and peace are dwindling.

However, in our country Bhutan, the flourishing of the precious tradition of Buddha dharma has been the fount of peace, happiness and security. As a result of this sacred covenant, apart from a vibrant and verdant ecology, there is a wealth of kindness, compassion and a moral sense of poetic justice naturally rich in all the people.

Because of these qualities inherent in our society, religious and political goodwill and success are increasing like the waxing moon. Therefore, there is little conflict, hunger and ailment. Since the security, happiness and peace we enjoy are comparable to ancient days of fortunate generations, Bhutan has become an object of global admiration and commendation.

I see an immense benefit to the nation in *Bhutan Observer*'s initiative to bring out a magazine on the Buddhist theme. I commend the paper's noble initiative and earnestly pray that the magazine is of great benefit to all human beings.

Issued from Tashichhodzong on the 30th day of the 6th month of the Earth Female Ox year in the 17th Rabjung.

Truelku Jigme Choeda the 70th Je Khenpo of Bhutan

This is the ultimate seal of approval for our magazine. I am agog.

17

Dolma's Story

If the world practised what Bhutan preached, we might be in better shape. But despite the country's aspirations, every day the newspapers show the kingdom has a long way to go to achieve its own ideals. Reality hurts. Health figures are published and the kingdom's problem with alcoholism is laid bare. Corruption of high-level civil servants is revealed. A business consortium, including a royal in-law, is denounced for building dodgy roads. The royal is never mentioned, but newspaper readers know who it is and the story becomes a touchy subject. The Bhutanese do not like to see their heroes, particularly their royal family, diminished. It diminishes them all.

I first hear about domestic violence through Fiona Stiedl, who volunteers at the new women's shelter RENEW, which stands for Respect, Educate, Nurture and Empower Women. Fiona is a British psychologist and 'trailing spouse'. Her husband works with Megan at the Dutch aid agency SNV, and she volunteers her services as a counsellor where she is allowed.

RENEW was set up in 2004 by the youngest Queen after she travelled the country talking to women about the hardships of their lives, only to discover domestic abuse on an unimagined scale. RENEW estimates that a staggering 75 per cent of Bhutanese women are victims of violence in their own homes.

After Fiona tells me this figure, I spend weeks trying to get my head around it. I bristle in an editorial conference as the male editors pontificate about Bhutan's unique vision for Gross National Happiness. Three in four Bhutanese women might not be feeling so happy. I listen as the editors earnestly discuss poverty and the hardships faced by their rural cousins, and how they can find a way to help. Not these husbands, surely. I know wife-beaters don't have signs tattooed on their forehead, but still. It just will not compute.

Then one morning in February, our helper, Dolma, doesn't come to work.

Mal rings me at the newspaper to say she is in jail. She had a fight with her husband the previous night, police were called, and she ended up locked in a cell.

He found this out from Dolma's best friend, a young woman who works for our Dutch neighbour, Cecile. She tells us that Dolma's husband is violent when he drinks, which is often.

Cecile is a formidable woman who trained as a political scientist and could easily be Prime Minister of the Netherlands one day. She goes straight to the police station and gets Dolma out of jail. Once it becomes clear that Dolma is the injured party, the police do everything to help. They record an apology in the paperwork and haul in her husband, Arjun, for an official warning. The police captain berates him for his shameful behaviour. He tells Arjun to clear out his things from their apartment that afternoon.

Dolma comes back to Tashi Pelkhil village and spends the afternoon sleeping in our spare room. When I come home from work she is sitting in our kitchen, shoulders slumped, looking broken. Her whole body sags. I give her a hug and she is trembling. She is so ashamed of spending a night in jail that she can hardly speak.

Mal drives Dolma and her daughters home and walks them up the stairs to their apartment. It is locked from the inside. Arjun is home and at first refuses to let them in. Mal is polite but firm, and finally Arjun opens the door.

Arjun is a driver at a diplomatic office in Thimphu. He is small-framed, well spoken, neatly dressed and utterly charming. He doesn't look able to hurt a fly. Dolma tells us later that he is always like that to other people, which made her feel even more at fault and isolated.

Arjun refuses, ever so politely, to leave, so Mal calls the police. When they arrive, the police captain – who is still appalled that his officers put a beaten wife in jail – orders him from the home. The captain writes down his own mobile number for Dolma. Any more trouble and she is to call him, day or night.

The next morning Dolma arrives looking tired but determined. She asks if we can all sit down in the lounge room. She is tense, and it clearly takes enormous effort to hold herself together. She apologises but says she has to resign. She must go to Israel, where her sister works as a maid. Her sister will lend her money for the airfare and help her get a similar job. She hopes to send money home to educate her daughters.

Mal and I listen in shock. She has made up her mind, she says. She has already told her daughters. They are upset and don't want her to go, but she has to. Her husband is a violent drunk. She cannot rely on him. This is the only way she can see to pay for her daughters' education, to give them a future better than hers.

Dolma was born in Thimphu to parents of Nepalese origin who were working on the roads. They were illiterate and did not register her birth with the village headman. That makes her part of a Bhutanese underclass, with almost no rights. When her beautiful daughters, who are bright and excelling at school, start Year 10, they will no longer be eligible for free education, because Dolma is not legally Bhutanese.

She will have to pay, and to afford that she must go to Israel to work as a maid, like her sister.

The idea that a mother must leave her children for a few years is devastating. One daughter is a year older than Kathryn, the other two years older. Leave them for a few years? Could I do the same, leave Kathryn for a few *years*? I know, in a vague way, that this happens. Europe is full of 'helpers' from Asia who send money to their families back home. More than 6 million Indonesians work as domestic help or labourers in overseas countries and send money home to their families. It is a figure that stuck in my head from a story I read recently. The number was shocking, and yet unreal. This is the first time a mother I know has sat on my couch and explained why leaving the children she so clearly loves – and leaving them in the care of a drunken, abusive father – is her best option. But without an education they have no future. This country has no welfare system or support mechanisms. Without legal rights or education, young women can face bleak choices.

Dolma's daughters are funny, bright and doing well at school. They are affectionate and respectful to Dolma, often standing with an arm draped around her shoulder. They love the Tashi books by Australian writer Anna Fienberg and JK Rowling's Harry Potter series, both on sale in Thimphu's largest bookshop. And Dolma is a devoted mother. Every day while I am at work, she and Mal share news about their children. How they are going at school, what they are reading, the myriad things they do each day that enthral a parent.

I see with stark clarity the powerlessness of an uneducated woman in a third-world country. But Dolma cannot leave her girls. That cannot possibly be good for anybody. Not her and not them.

Dolma is not seeking our help or charity or pity. She is telling us because we are her employers and she is resigning. Effective immediately. She plans to leave for Israel as soon as her sister can send money.

I suggest that she might be making a rash decision. Instead of going to Israel and leaving behind her children, there must be another way. We need to find out her rights. Even as I am saying it, I am aware it is a completely Western reaction. She looks at me blankly. Her rights?

The options available to me as an educated, middle-class Australian are not available to her. I cannot change her world and I realise it would be unfair to imply that I could. I feel completely out of my depth, and suggest we see Fiona at the new women's shelter – she will know what to do.

RENEW is in an impressive new four-storey building on the edge of town, half hidden from the street by other buildings. Central but discreet. It could be a new hotel. A plaque outside commemorates the organisation being founded in 2004 by Her Majesty the Queen, Ashi Sangay Choden Wangchuck. Fiona meets us and brings a RENEW caseworker, a beautifully groomed young Bhutanese woman. The four of us sit in an office and listen as Dolma tells of her violent 16-year marriage.

When Arjun was sober, he was charming – a good husband and father. When he drank, he spent all their money, told her she was worthless and beat her. She rubs her thigh as she talks, then explains that it constantly aches – the result of a beating seven months ago with a wooden roti stick, a thin rolling pin. She shows us bruises on her wrists and arms. As she speaks, every word seems to bring a wave of self-disgust, and tears drip off her cheeks onto her clasped hands.

RENEW recently ran an advertisement in *Bhutan Times* with the message 'Home is a place for love and happiness, not violence', beside a disturbing picture of a child cowering in a corner while a man in a *gho* raises his fist to a woman who is shielding her face.

But women like Dolma, who are uneducated, do not read newspapers. That the violence is not her fault is news to her. After 16 years of abuse, she has absorbed the blame for much of it. She is unaware that it is against the law for Arjun to beat her if he does not like his dinner. That the youngest Queen Mother has set up an organisation specifically to help women in the same situation is a bewildering revelation.

RENEW is well funded and branches are opening up across the country. I am told that while there are men in powerful positions who champion the organisation, there are others who object to any interference in the home. Marriages, they say, are private business.

Bhutan is where Australia was 30 to 35 years ago. Back then, domestic violence was a hidden crime, seldom reported. It was only in the 1970s, when second-wave feminists began to expose its extent, that the community addressed it. There is still a long way to go: recent statistics show that 23 per cent of Australian women have experienced domestic violence in their lifetime.

In Bhutan, change is coming not from women's liberation but from the government. It isn't a grassroots movement, and it's not even coming from the educated middle class. It is being imposed from the top, like democracy. Improving the status and protection of women is one of the United Nations Millennium Development Goals, and the UN has provided funding for the Bhutanese government to create a National Commission for Women and Children (NCWC). Its head, Dr Rinchen Chophel, is a fierce advocate for women's rights, appearing often on BBS and in the newspapers as he argues for the abolishment of traditions that disadvantage women. His current list of battles includes bolstering the rights of single mothers and shifting the legal blame from sex workers to their clients.

Dr Chophel also set up the Woman and Child Protection Unit in Royal Bhutan Police. The unit is headed by Lieutenant Karma Rigzin, a well-known and highly respected figure in the country. Fiona tells me that the staff at RENEW just have to pick up the phone to her, and her officers will appear. She is known to 'kick ass'. Her name comes up frequently in the editorial conferences at *Bhutan Observer.* Three of the four editors dated her and seem keen to mention it at every opportunity. I understand why when I see a photo of her posing in her police uniform with her male officers behind her. She looks beautiful. And tough.

NCWC and RENEW advertise in the media, and the newspapers report on their work. The reporters interview abused women, changing their names and concealing their faces in photos as they detail heartbreaking stories.

While the educated Bhutanese are shocked by the coverage, the limited penetration of newspapers means it is taking time for such an important message to filter through to all levels of society. But it is a start. Domestic violence is a boil that needs to be lanced. The result is painful and ugly, but necessary.

It is clear that a contributing factor to the problem of domestic violence is alcohol. Bhutan has a strong culture of drinking. Cheap whisky is freely available in Thimphu shops, and every Bhutanese farmer knows how to brew *ara*, a potent liquor made from rice. It is served to guests on special occasions, warmed in a saucepan, with an egg floating in it. *Ara* is so much a part of rural culture that life without it is inconceivable.

Fiona and the RENEW caseworker recommend that Dolma see the forensic doctor at Thimphu hospital to have her scars and injuries recorded in preparation for a divorce. Unless she can prove he is at fault, she will have to pay for the privilege of divorcing him. The forensic doctor is professional, kind and clearly used to seeing women like Dolma.

He draws pictures of her injuries on a piece of paper, adds comments and clips it into a thick ring-bound folder, which he places next to a row of a dozen similar folders. 'Battered Wifes' is handwritten on each spine. Pinned to the walls are posters saying domestic violence is a crime. They are in English and Dzongkha, neither of which Dolma can read.

I bump into a Bhutanese friend. She tells me she has been waiting next door for test results. In the past hour four battered women have visited this room. One had a savage bite mark on her arm. My friend shakes her head. 'Her husband *bit* her,' she whispers.

Dolma takes a week off and goes to visit her parents, an eight-hour bus journey away. When she returns she is buoyant, like her old self. She had a wonderful break, she tells us. Her mother, who is paralysed, took a few steps on her own, so everyone in the family is rejoicing.

Dolma told her parents she was divorcing Arjun. They thought that was a mistake and advised her she should allow him to return, even if just for a few years.

She says it so cheerfully that at first I miss it. Her parents want her to go back to him? *For a few years?*

Dolma explains that she doesn't have Bhutanese citizenship. Even though she was born in Thimphu, to parents who were in the country legitimately, she is not registered anywhere and is thus considered an illegal immigrant. Nepal has refugee camps full of people who claim they are Bhutanese but cannot prove it and have been kicked out of the country. They are stateless. Dolma knows this could be her future. Living in a refugee camp, unable to help her daughters.

Arjun, however, comes from a well-connected family, which is partly why Dolma's parents think she is better off with him, violent or not. Arjun's father was a decorated army officer, and Arjun himself has level-five citizenship, which will be upgraded in a few months to level four. This is when I first learn about the hierarchy around me – that Bhutanese citizenship covers five levels. Good for you if your family exists in level one – born in Bhutan to Bhutanese ancestors who owned land that was registered with the local government office and whose extended family has never been in trouble with the law or the government. That seems to be a rough definition of it: no two Bhutanese give me the same explanation and it quickly becomes clear that this is another conversation that is impolite for a foreigner to be having.

An expat friend warns me to be careful. Foreigners are tolerated, but rock the boat and your visa will be quietly cancelled. It could also draw unwelcome attention to Dolma. The refugee camps are a thorny issue. So is citizenship. So are foreigners.

A new RENEW caseworker tells us that Dolma can apply for citizenship, but it will take 20 years from the day of her application. And she must pass a written Dzongkha test. Dolma never went to school and, like half the people in Thimphu and three-quarters of Bhutan, speaks little Dzongkha. It seems an impossible and unfair hurdle.

But the good news is that her children are learning Dzongkha at school and, with their father's level-four citizenship, they can sit the test at 16 and be registered as Bhutanese citizens. Level five. At least Dolma won't have to go to Israel to fund their education.

The caseworker tells us there is one way that Dolma can side-step the 20-year wait. A marriage certificate. Unfortunately, Dolma doesn't have one. Like most Bhutanese, she and Arjun just set up house together. Wedding ceremonies are for rich people. But if she can get the headman, the *gup*, in Arjun's village to write down that to his knowledge they have been married for the past 16 years, it will suffice.

A few days after returning, Dolma tells me that Arjun is very, very sorry for putting her in jail. He knows he went too far. He is ashamed. He has promised to stop drinking and assures her that if he breaks his promise, she can throw him out. Dolma says she believes him. She wants to give him another chance. It is better to take her husband back – for the children and her citizenship.

She asks if I am disappointed with her, and my heart sinks. Dolma was born here, has lived her whole life here, but feels more secure in an abusive marriage than out of it, on her own. Her choices seem so woefully limited. I do not share her optimism, but it is not up to me.

I tell her I think she looks like a woman in control and that has to be good.

I have had virtually nothing to do with domestic violence in my own life and yet I discover I seem to know an awful lot about it. When Dolma says Arjun will change, a voice in my head says 'it won't happen'. I wonder how I know that. It seems that women's rights and the cycle of abuse is so much a part of the Australian media landscape – through advertisements and newspaper stories, even Hollywood movies – that I have absorbed much about it by osmosis. Dolma didn't even know it had a name.

I cross my fingers and hope that I am wrong.

For the first month Arjun stays sober. Each day Mal and I breathe a sigh of relief when we see Dolma walking into Tashi Pelkhil village with the other helpers. After two months Dolma quietly asks if she can hide her jewellery under our mattress. Mal and I watch on, our hearts in our mouths.

Then one night, three months after her husband put her in jail, Dolma phones Mal on his mobile. She is hysterical. Arjun is drunk and going berserk. Her daughters have fled to a neighbour's home.

Mal drives the ten minutes to her apartment. Dolma opens the door, her face puffy. Arjun is immediately polite, half bowing to Mal, both hands out, palms upward in Bhutanese greeting. But it doesn't last long. He's too drunk to maintain the charade. He launches himself at Dolma, calling her a slut, but Mal steps between them.

Arjun tries to talk to him. 'My wife is a slut,' he tells Mal. 'She has slept with other men.'

We know a little of Dolma's story and it is not pretty. She was 12 when she left her parents and moved in with a rich family as a maid. She was not a virgin when she left, some years later. She was about 18 when she married Arjun and has always been faithful to him, but when he drinks he accuses her of sleeping around.

'How would *you* feel if your wife had slept with other men?' Arjun screams at Mal.

'I know she has,' says Mal. 'So what?'

Arjun stops dead in his tracks, mouth open, staring.

'Before she met me, she slept with other men,' continues Mal. 'Is that what this is about? After 16 years of marriage you're upset about a man she may have slept with before you were married? So you hit her?'

Mal calls him a 'pathetic little man'.

Arjun objects. 'You have no right to interfere.'

'I'm here protecting your wife and your daughters from you,' says Mal coldly.

Arjun ignores him and lunges at Dolma, calling her a slut and worse, much worse. Mal steps in front. Arjun is small, drunk and angry. Mal is over six feet tall, sober and deadly calm. It's not an even match. Arjun bounces off Mal's chest. Without getting into a full fistfight, they keep up this strange boxing bout around the living room with Mal keeping Arjun away from both Dolma and the kitchen – where there are knives – until the police arrive.

They take Arjun to the station and lock him up. Then they take statements from Mal, Dolma's friend, Dolma and the two girls. One daughter tells of how she locked herself in the toilet and her father tried to bash down the door. She says she was very scared.

Dolma sits with the girls, helping them make their statements. Mal finally stumbles home at 1.30 am, exhausted. Kathryn has taken his spot in our bed, so he gets into hers. His feet stick out the end and his head is on her elephant pillow. Mickey Mouse dances across the doona that covers him. It's a different version of masculinity from Arjun's, and the sight brings a lump to my throat.

We don't see Dolma for a few days, and when she comes, she'll talk to me but cannot bring herself even to look at Mal. She tells me she is grateful to him but so shamed by what her husband told him. The language, the insults. She is humiliated. I try to reassure her that Mal doesn't think that way.

Dolma says she feels supported and protected – by Mal and me, the police, the girls; even Arjun's parents have sided with her against their son. But the ramifications of Arjun's arrest are a disaster. There is no going back this time and, with a divorce pending, no way she can get a marriage certificate. Without that, Dolma cannot get citizenship.

I find the caseworker at RENEW starts to be less helpful. She says Dolma is committing a crime just by living here. Every day she doesn't register with Immigration, she is committing an illegal act. But, I argue, if she does go to Immigration, they could deport her. Take her to the Indian border and deposit her on the other side, away from her children, never allowed back again.

To me, it's only a matter of paperwork, but it becomes clear that the caseworker sees it differently. In her eyes Dolma is not Bhutanese. The fact that she has lived here since birth is irrelevant.

'You don't want illegal immigrants in your country, do you?' she asks me, with a distinct edge to her voice.

I bite my tongue.

If only we could prove she has been here all these years. I mention the family for whom Dolma worked as a 12-year-old. One family member is a retired government minister. Would a letter from him help?

The caseworker looks horrified. It is illegal to employ an underage worker. They would be admitting to a crime.

What if they said she merely lived with their family?

'It is a crime to have an illegal immigrant live with you.' She says Dolma's only hope is a marriage certificate.

I explain the marriage has broken down irretrievably. The caseworker sighs deeply, as if Dolma has done this deliberately to irritate her, then says she will need to seek further advice.

And so begins months of advice and counter-advice, all of it bewildering. Dr Chophel, the head of the NCWC, is kindly and goes out of his way to help. Dolma has tears in her eyes when she recounts how well he treated her when she visited him in his office. I feel humbled that it is such a novelty for her to be shown respect from an important person.

But for every person on Dolma's side, there is another who treats her like a criminal. She travels for days across the country to visit a *gup* who might be able to give her a piece of paper that would confirm she exists, only to have him refuse to see her.

Seeing the world through Dolma's eyes changes something irrevocably. I am shocked by her precarious identity, her disempowerment because she cannot read, her lack of rights as a woman in an underclass in a third-world country.

Suddenly the stories in *Bhutan Observer* affect me more. It is not just the plight of the women, desperate though that often is. It is rural poverty. Families going without food in winter; parents sending their five-year-olds to walk through snow for two hours to get to school; nuns as young as seven going to the toilet in the forest at night, terrified by the wild animals; boy monks who die from malnutrition; children working in fields or as maids in rich homes; and Layap girls being married off at 12.

They are all Dolma and Dolma is me, and somehow it is all more real and heartbreaking than it was a month ago. The stories in the newspaper hurt in a way they didn't before. I feel raw and angry and humbled and wretched. It is too much. I want to go home. And yet I cannot imagine ever going home, to real-estate prices and culture wars and reality TV.

These feelings arise in all the foreigners who stay here beyond a two-week trek. They see what the tourists don't and inevitably it comes as a shock. A punch in the guts.

The narrative of Bhutan is Shangri-La and Gross National Happiness. It is mystical, utopian and an antidote to the errors of the modern world. It is what the Bhutanese want their country to be and it is what I want it to be. When the myth is shattered, it hurts.

Fiona tells me the tragic story of two young teenage girls at RENEW who are pregnant as a result of incest. Their mothers have disowned them and they cannot return to their villages. They are just schoolgirls.

She describes a woman beaten by her husband so severely she is now brain-damaged. Like Dolma, she did not have citizenship and he thought she could not complain. Lieutenant Karma set him straight. Men are not allowed to beat anyone, citizen or non-citizen.

A nurse tells of a young woman who died a slow agonising death in the men's ward after an overdose of paracetamol tablets. Her husband had taken a second wife. When the hospital telephoned the husband, the new wife told them to go away.

The stories go on. This is not Shangri-La. It is as flawed as any other country. And, as foreigners, we are not supposed to see these things or interfere. We are supposed to admire the country for its ideal of Gross National Happiness, then we are supposed to go home, back to our bloated first-world lives.

18

Two Remarkable Women

The role of women in Bhutan is complicated and contradictory. Inheritance law means that daughters generally inherit the family farm, while sons are left to fend for themselves. But in positions of authority, women are poorly represented. There are no women in the 11-member government cabinet, and just six in the 25-member National Council. The ones who do make it to positions of authority, such as Lieutenant Karma Rigzin, are highly respected.

Other powerful women in Bhutan include the pilot Ugyen Dema, the judge Namgay Peldon, and Bhutan Broadcasting Service's managing director, Pema Choden. She is an ex-diplomat, married to a former monk who gave up his vows and robes to be with her. He now takes tourists on treks while she runs BBS, managing the staff and budgets. She has launched an online radio station and speaks knowledgeably at communications forums around the globe.

But the most important woman in the whole country is the legendary Neten Zangmo. The Fourth King appointed Neten Zangmo to the toughest job in Bhutan – the head of the Anti-Corruption Commission (ACC). Part of her job is to re-educate the public about what constitutes corruption now that their country is a democracy.

She regularly runs newspaper advertising campaigns that explain different forms of corruption. Certain cultural traditions, such as nepotism, ignoring illegal acts to save face and giving gifts to officials, are no longer acceptable. In fact, they are against the law.

Neten Zangmo and her team publish the *ACC Quarterly News Update*, a two-page newsletter inserted in the newspapers. It includes a column by an eminent spiritual master explaining how karma works on the corrupt.

Like everything else to do with democracy, the new rules of business and civic responsibility require some getting used to. According to Bhutanese friends, practices that Neten Zangmo says are no longer allowed are so entrenched in the society that people won't know how to do business without them. Others will disregard the laws, believing themselves to be above them, which is probably understandable because until democracy, people of high status often *were* above the law. Not anymore. Such practices now have a name – corruption. But in this rigidly hierarchical society, not everyone thinks corruption is a big deal. It is the way things have always been done. An ACC survey on how the people feel about corruption shows that while it is prevalent – particularly bribes and nepotism among government employees – the Bhutanese do not think it is so bad. While the Fourth King, the Fifth King, the government and Neten Zangmo take it very seriously, the community shows remarkable tolerance. *Bhutan Observer* reports that corruption 'does not carry a heavy social stigma in Bhutan, according to an Anti-Corruption Commission survey. To be known as a corrupt person in Bhutan is not generally viewed as a great or lasting shame.'

This tolerance comes partly from a culture of unquestioning respect for superiors and partly from Buddhist beliefs. Everyone will reap their own karma. An old Dzongkha saying is, 'There is no person without faults; there is no tree without knots.' Buddhism doesn't carry notions of revenge or punishment. Instead, it encourages compassion for those human afflictions, such as greed and ignorance, which we all have. When leaders are caught out, many Bhutanese prefer to leave them be, not shame them further.

But Neten Zangmo has declared war on corruption and she is fearless. This petite, bespectacled woman faces off against business leaders, bureaucrats and government ministers. She has taken some of Bhutan's most high-profile people to court and made powerful enemies.

It is a lonely job. Every day she faces abuse and threats from people she is investigating. But she has even more powerful supporters. After *Bhutan Times* publishes a particularly bruising round of criticism from some powerful businessmen, the Fifth King steps in. He doesn't say anything directly or interfere in any way: rather, he bestows on her the red scarf, publicly applauding her tenacity and integrity. It is the equivalent of a knighthood and comes with a medal and the title of Dasho. She is the country's first female Dasho.

The Fifth King's support is sublimely effective. Newspapers immediately run long profile pieces celebrating the achievements of this remarkable woman. Readers write in with their Neten Zangmo stories. *Bhutan Times* calls her the 'Heart Daughter of Bhutan'. And the businessmen quietly shut up.

Neten Zangmo is like a friend to *Bhutan Observer*, having been a member of the initial conclave to determine the newspaper's direction. She is part of the ongoing discussion with the proprietors about how the newspaper can best exemplify Gross National Happiness. In news conferences the editors speak of her reverentially.

Neten Zangmo has been a legend in our home for years. Mal has admired her over his two decades of visiting Bhutan with Dzongsar Khyentse Rinpoche. When Mal first met her she was the principal of a technical college. He thought she was gutsy and fun then. Mal introduced me to her at a party in 2002 during the making of *Travellers & Magicians*. She sat on the floor, explaining the country's constitution, which she was helping to draft. She was formidably intelligent, but also cheeky and cheerful. After the Fifth King awarded her the red scarf, *Kuensel* wrote, 'She is seltzer with a lifetime fizz … She is the antithesis of the packaged leader – irrepressible, candid, spontaneous, funny, feisty, independent, unfashionable and strangely charismatic – a woman oddly at peace with herself in one of the country's most sensitive institutions. She is, clearly, an original.'

Befitting her esteemed position as a Dasho and the head of the ACC, Neten Zangmo has a toilet attached to her office. But in keeping with her own principles, she insists on cleaning it herself. She often features in *Bhutan Observer*'s political cartoons, usually depicted wearing a *kira* and Nikes, chasing some corrupt person down the street.

Another Bhutanese woman who makes her way into the pages of *Bhutan Observer* exists at the other end of the social scale. Rita lives with her husband and four children in a toilet block opposite the newspaper's office. I watch them from my window. When I find out the small white-washed building I pass every day is both their home and a public toilet, I am shocked, but also fascinated by the family.

The mother is voluptuous in vivid Indian saris, and has a jolly sense of humour. She washes the children in a bucket of cold water on the footpath while they wail and scream. She hangs wet laundry on the street fence as her children play in the gutter.

One daughter, who is about the same age as Kathryn, greets me every morning. She is a chatterbox, but not in English. Even though I understand little of what she is saying, I look forward to seeing her. Her smile lights up the street.

I start bringing her small gifts – colouring pencils and, as it gets colder, some of Kathryn's winter clothes. I feel ridiculously pleased when I see her wearing the mittens and boots, striding up and down the street pretending to be a soldier. I think that means she likes them.

Needrup announces in our news conference that he wants profiles about real people to balance all the coverage of 'important' people, and I suggest the family in the toilet. Everyone in the room immediately knows who I mean. We all pass them every morning. Needrup likes the idea and appoints Metho Dema, a sweet, dreamy 21-year-old reporter, to do the story. She lets me tag along.

We go after lunch and discover that the family is having a siesta. Rita, the mother, doesn't mind our intrusion. This is a public toilet and they have visitors all day.

There are four cubicles for men and four for women, none with doors. A corridor separates them from view and from the family but there is an open drain, so the smell of urine and excrement hangs heavily over us. The family has two small rooms of their own. One is the size of a toilet cubicle with a gas ring for cooking. The other has a queen-size mattress that touches three of the walls, leaving only about half a square metre of the floor for the whole family to live, eat and sleep. On a shelf, a rented television shows Hindi soapies. Pinned to the grimy walls are posters of Hindu gods.

Metho explains that we are from *Bhutan Observer* and would like to write a story about her family. Rita looks surprised but shyly agrees. She sits in the middle of the mattress, a tangle of sleeping children's limbs on and around her. I watch in admiration as Metho slips into Hindi and draws out Rita's story, taking notes and translating as she goes.

Rita is 30 and was born in Bengal, India. Her father, a sweeper with Thimphu City Corporation, was hurt by a bomb blast. He is now partially blind with an injured hand, so he cannot work. He lives in the border town of Phuentsholing, about seven hours' drive away. Because the bomb blast was on government premises, Rita and her family are allowed to live rent-free in these rooms. Even with the language barrier I can hear the pride in her voice as she gestures around her.

Rita acts as caretaker and the people who use the toilet give her a few ngultrum. It can add up to Nu.30–40 a day (A$1), which she says helps. The people are kind and sometimes give Nu.5 (A$0.14) to the children. The family's main income, though, is from sweeping: Rita sweeps a local office block and her husband sweeps government offices. The family – two adults and four children – shares this queen-size mattress.

Rita tells Metho that she sees me going to work each day. She smiles at me. I say I like her children; they always seem to be having fun. She explains they are sleeping now because they are tired after their cold bucket bath that morning.

She is chatty and warm, a woman comfortable in her own skin and her own home. She talks about her husband. It was an arranged marriage. They came to Thimphu when their eldest child was just three months old. He is a good man, strict with the children when he is around. They are a handful when he is away.

Metho asks if there is anything I would like to ask. We have a short discussion in English about the fact that this woman and her family live in a toilet block. Metho is as shocked by this as me. We discuss that what we really want to know is if she is happy living here. But how do you ask that without implying you don't think she should be?

Metho thinks for a moment, then turns to Rita and they talk for a few minutes. When Metho turns back to me she is grinning.

'She feels privileged to have a home. She says the people who sweep the roads don't have homes and she knows how incredibly lucky she is. Her oldest children are going to school and she wants them to learn Dzongkha. Her dream is that all her children grow up in Bhutan, become educated and learn Dzongkha. She doesn't want to go back to India because there is no work. Here she has a home and work. She says she is really content with her life.'

Rita adds something in Hindi and Metho translates.

'She says if you have more you just want more.'

Rita gives a huge broad smile.

On the way back to the office, Metho marvels at Rita. She has walked past the family for the six months she has worked at *Bhutan Observer* and not given her much thought. Now she considers her a revelation.

She writes a lovely feature for the next edition, which appears under the headline 'The happy little home', ending with Rita's sage-like advice, which struck such a chord with Metho. 'Her answer is a reminder that the secret of contentment is knowing how to enjoy what one has,' she writes.

After meeting Rita I stop thinking of them as the 'poor family in the toilet'. I find myself watching them and wondering about the nature of poverty and happiness, and about attitude. Rita's attitude. My attitude. The difference between feeling pity and having empathy. When I feel content, and when I feel like I don't have enough. It feels like a slippery measure that has me at one end one day and the opposite end on another day. I remember Krishnamurti, the Indian philosopher, talking about the evils of comparison. He said comparison was degrading and perverted one's outlook. I ponder what it might be like never to compare or be compared. The idea that they are poor but happy irritates me. There is so much poverty around me – grinding, heartbreaking, demoralising poverty – and by no stretch of the imagination can it be good to be poor. Still, Rita doesn't seem to think in terms of poor or not poor, and I should not impose them on her. It is patronising. And limiting. Wrong in ways I am just beginning to glimpse.

The confusion swirls around inside my head. I do not come up with any profound insights. But after meeting Rita and her family, and seeing their lives through their eyes, I start to realise how much

I perceive the world through my preconceptions. It prevents me from seeing anything as it might really be. I decide that everything I think I know could very well be wrong. And I cannot begin to explain why that makes me happy.

19

Forbidden Topics

On 13 March 2009, a 46-year-old woman is beaten to death by a mob of 14 villagers who believe she is possessed by Satan. While her husband and two daughters watch, the woman is beaten with a bamboo stick and spade handle. Villagers then tie a rope around her neck and hang her from an orange tree.

The villagers, from Dorokha, had recently converted to Christianity and were attending a prayer meeting in their pastor's farmhouse. They decided to kill the mother of five because she would not convert and was therefore clearly possessed by Satan. It was a massive frenzy of bloodlust unlike anything Bhutan had ever seen. According to *Kuensel*:

> Dorokha police said that most of the members of the group were 'acting like mad, putting the bible on their heads, staring at us, shouting at us'. 'They looked very frightening and they shouted at us "you are evil too and you will be put to death very soon, etc.",' said a Dorokha police constable. 'We had to get the help of local leaders and about 18 village volunteers to escort the accused group to Samtse,' he said.

The brutal event shocked Bhutan, but it was also seen by many to be inevitable. *That's what Christians do.* Siok Sian Pek-Dorji tells me that the modern experience of Christianity on this continent is often the hellfire-and-brimstone preachers who exhort sinners to repent or be damned. They are religious extremists inflaming rural communities. India and Nepal have wrestled with religious violence and scenes like the Dorokha killing since the early 20th century, when missionaries started coming from Europe to save their souls.

Christianity is a vexed issue in this kingdom with its new constitution, which guarantees 'freedom of thought, conscience and religion' but also states that 'Buddhism is the spiritual heritage of Bhutan, which promotes the principles and values of peace, non-violence, compassion and tolerance'. Roughly three-quarters of the country consider themselves Buddhist, about one quarter of the population is Hindu, and a small number have converted to Christianity. Islam is almost negligible, and Judaism doesn't figure at all, except perhaps among the expat community.

What this means in practice is that Hinduism happily coexists with Buddhism in Bhutan. There are Hindu temples in Thimphu and throughout the south, and the whole country joins in some of their religious holidays. The Bhutanese also have no problem with Islam, small as it is. Only Christianity is a struggle.

In some respects, Christianity has a good reputation. A Canadian Jesuit priest, Father William Mackey, is widely credited with bringing modern education into the country. He was a headmaster in India in the 1960s when he fell out with the country's leaders and was to be deported. The Third King invited him to Bhutan to establish an education system, but set one condition: that the priest would not try to convert anybody. Father Mackey agreed. He moved to Bhutan and stayed for 30 years. He established a modern school system and, true to his word, did not try to convert anyone to Catholicism. When he died in Thimphu in 1995, he was commemorated as a much-loved figure.

Father Mackey's non-aggressive version of Christianity is welcomed. And the Bhutanese who convert to Christianity when they travel abroad to study are free to practise it when they come home. What they are not allowed to do is try to convert anyone else. Bhutan's constitution expressly forbids pressuring people to convert. 'No person shall be compelled to belong to another faith by means of coercion or inducement.'

Missionaries are refused visas, though they still get in, coming across the border from India to liberate the Bhutanese from their supposed spiritual darkness. It is this type of evangelical Christianity – spreading the word of Christ, saving sinners, bringing others to God – that conflicts with Bhutan's culture. These Christians are supposed to 'save' everybody else, as they believe it would be lacking compassion to leave others on a path that is taking them straight to hell, but that view is incompatible with Bhutan's own ideal of tolerance.

Prime Minister Jigmi Y Thinley explained it succinctly in an interview with Christian organisation Compass:

> I view conversions very negatively, because conversion is the worst form of intolerance. The first premise is that you believe that your religion is the right religion, and the religion of the convertee is wrong – what he believes in is wrong, what he practises is wrong, that your religion is superior and that you have this responsibility to promote your way of life, your way of thinking, your way of worship. It is the worst form of intolerance. And it divides families and societies.
>
> Any kind of proselytisation that involves economic and material incentives [is wrong]. Many people are being converted on hospital beds in their weakest and most vulnerable moments. And these people are whispering in their ears that 'there is no hope for you. The only way that you can survive is if you accept this particular religion.' That is wrong.

The Prime Minister says Christians misunderstand Buddhism, specifically the icons and statues, which they see as false idols. To Buddhists, however, these icons represent different aspects of their own mind, and are inherently empty of any substance.

'To say that, "Your religion is wrong, worshipping idols is wrong" … who worships idols? We don't worship idols. Those are just representations and manifestations that help you to focus,' he says.

Last year a man was sentenced to three years' jail on proselytising charges for preaching and screening movies on Christianity in two villages. He was accused of attempting to promote civil unrest. The length of the sentence shows how seriously the authorities view such behaviour.

This kind of response to evangelical Christianity has landed Bhutanese on international Christian watchlists. The organisation Gospelgo, which is based in India, has accused Bhutan of 'Talibanizing its Christian population'.

The Dorokha Christian killing is reported on, discussed and analysed in the newspapers as Bhutanese try to wrestle with the issues it raises. What does the constitution say about religion? What is tolerance? Are churches banned? This public discussion is a first for Bhutan. Christianity has been one of the no-go areas for the Bhutanese media.

As far as I can tell, there are four such topics in Bhutan. Anything negative about the Kings and the royal family; the refugees from southern Bhutan; the sometimes-flexible borders with China; and Christianity. On these sensitive matters, there has been virtually no public discussion. Once again, it is not the government or the Kings who keep these issues out of the newspapers. They do not telephone the proprietors and have a quiet word. It is the editors themselves who do not give them oxygen. In the same way they understand their readers do not want to read gossip or anything else negative about their Kings, they also understand what will and won't work within their society.

The fact that Christianity is being openly discussed in the pages of the newspapers indicates the beginning of an opening, a loosening up, part of the freedom brought by democracy. The editors-in-chief have not sought permission from anyone to start publishing commentary about Christianity. They sensed the time was right. The circumstances of the country have changed.

The situation with the borders are considered to be a matter of national security, but the refugee issue, after decades of silence, could be next to find its way into the pages of the newspapers. It is due to be discussed in parliament, along with citizenship, so it will inevitably be reported and move into public discussion.

In the 1980s, Bhutan was facing a growing problem in the south among their Lhotshampa population, who are of Nepalese ethnicity. After decades of living in the region and raising families, some had integrated with the Bhutanese way of life and some hadn't. More arrived illegally, fleeing poverty in Nepal. As numbers grew, some southern Bhutanese wanted more official representation of their Nepalese culture. Tensions culminated in terrorist bombings and clashes with the Royal Bhutan Army.

People needed to be able to prove they or their family had lived in Bhutan before 1958. According to the international press, some of the police and local government officials who enacted the new laws were bullies and corrupt, and they report shocking stories of brutality, which go unreported inside Bhutan. Fearing for their safety, 100,000 Nepalese-speaking southern Bhutanese fled to Nepal, where they spent the next 15 years in UN refugee camps. All of them have since been resettled in countries including the USA, Canada, Australia, Norway and Denmark.

As a foreigner, it is hard to make sense of how the Bhutanese feel about it now. It seems there is lingering confusion, anger, shame and fear. The issue is not discussed with foreigners and not mentioned in the media.

Dolma is one result of the policies. She lives in an awful state of non-citizenship, scared she could be deported any day. But in the newspaper office are half-a-dozen journalists and advertising staff from southern Bhutan who have integrated completely. They consider themselves thoroughly Bhutanese, from the hems of their *ghos* to the edges of their *kabneys*. I also come across southern Bhutanese Hindus of Nepalese descent in the civil service, business community and monasteries.

But still that tumultuous time casts a pall. For the Bhutanese, it is the elephant in the room, rarely discussed, but across the borders in Nepal it is a popular topic. The Nepalese media is scathing about Bhutan, sometimes to the point of hysteria.

Needrup goes to Kathmandu for a few days to attend an international media conference. He comes back bemused by discussions about Bhutan. He sat on a panel on the first day and told of his experience launching an independent newspaper and how democracy had just arrived in Bhutan. He was followed by a web journalist from a refugee camp in Nepal, who claimed the press in Bhutan was suppressed and the country had no judiciary. The Bhutan he described was not one Needrup recognised, and Needrup found himself in heated arguments with a number of journalists.

'A German woman wouldn't believe we weren't suppressed,' he tells me. 'I told the Bhutanese web journalist that they must stop printing untruths. It is the first tenet of journalism to tell the truth and they are not. They say we have no judiciary. We have a judiciary.

'There is self-censorship. But things are changing. A year ago we wouldn't have written about the Christian killings. That was a sensitive issue. In a year we will be writing about the refugee issue. We are openly critical of the government. The government doesn't tell us what to write. They don't sit on our shoulder.'

Perhaps understandably, it is hard for the press in Nepal to see beyond the traumatic experiences of the refugees. For them, it seems to define Bhutan, and as a result they make other, unfair judgments about Bhutan.

I understand Needrup's indignation. I have sat in on *Bhutan Observer* news conferences and observed the process from discussing a topic to pulling together a story – how it is edited, where it goes in the newspaper – then seeing the reaction from readers and how Needrup decides which letters to publish. I have been privy to how he and the editors make their decisions and the pressures they face. *Bhutan Observer* may have problems, including getting ministers to talk to them, but government interference in what they publish is not one of them. Even in its infancy, the relationship between the government and growing independent media is robust.

I also appreciate what Needrup means by self-censorship. Every editor everywhere in the world does it. Obviously, the better an editor understands their readers' sensibilities, the more successful they are as an editor. The *Bhutan Times* editors have been learning the hard way, through incidents such as the public outcry after they published the photograph of the dead foetus. But self-censorship is complicated and, in this small society where everybody knows everybody, it requires a particular skill. I ask Kinley Dorji what it was like when there was only *Kuensel*. Was he censored? He tells me of a story he spiked many years ago, about the director of the Department of Livestock.

'I knew he was the best director we could have. Bhutan had a small pool of people who know about livestock. Then he went and messed up a project. Messed it up completely. I knew that if I wrote the story the Fourth King would read it and the man would lose his job. And I knew he was the best person to do that job. So what to do? Is it truth at all costs? We had all the proof. But at that stage

I knew he was the second person trained in livestock in the whole country. If he went, who would replace him? A civil servant who had no clue about livestock planning? So I made the decision not to run the story.'

He says the topic came up when he was doing his master's degree at Columbia. 'I discussed this in a class. Some kids said, "You had to write it, it is the truth. It happened." But I was in a different situation. I had a different level of responsibility.

'I remember the Columbia professor, a former journalist, said that this is the problem. In our search for the truth we ignore our responsibilities. It's a decision we actually have to make. In a newspaper hierarchy, of course a reporter doesn't think of all those things. But as you grow older and become more senior in an organisation you do have to start to think about those wider implications. You start making broader decisions.

'Self-censorship is a very powerful, complex culture. It is beyond journalism. We all do it day to day in our lives. As an editor you ... sometimes read between the lines, sometimes don't mention things, for a greater good. Is it nothing but the truth or is there a bigger truth? There are perspectives.'

He explains that the censorship decisions he made as an editor came from understanding the sensibilities of Bhutanese society.

'You don't criticise the King. I guess in many ways we were criticising the King because he was head of government and we were criticising the government. But we didn't criticise the King directly. It's not that the King would get angry and put us in jail. It's because Bhutanese society wouldn't be able to take it. They have made that very clear. The Bhutanese people would get very, very hurt.'

Kinley recounts an incident where a Dutch newspaper wrote an unfavourable piece about the Fourth King. Angry people called *Kuensel* and asked them to do something about it. 'I heard the King's reaction to the story was to laugh. He said, "It took them a long time to write something like this." That was it. But the Bhutanese people weren't laughing. They were very hurt and angry.'

Bhutan Today runs an editorial criticising the process of *kidu*. It is the nearest thing to openly criticising His Majesty and it causes quite a stir. Like the photo of the bloody foetus, this story is considered in extreme poor taste. It has crossed a line the Bhutanese do not want crossed. The *Bhutan Today* editor is Indian, and various journalists tell me that a Bhutanese editor would have known better, that this error of judgment shows why foreigners should not be allowed to hold positions of influence. They do not understand local sensitivities.

Siok Sian Pek-Dorji says: 'The market freedom we have is startling. We call the kettle black. You don't have to name names in a small society. Everyone knows. You have to master the art of writing in a way that everyone understands. You have more effect that way. Self-censorship comes from understanding your culture. By not naming people, not stating it, people in Bhutan understand.'

20

Brand Bhutan

Bhutan Observer's receptionist understands little English and my Sharchop is not improving. We have parallel conversations, which I've come to enjoy as a suitably absurd start to the day. I ask for a paper-clip, and she tells me the time. When I admire her *kira*, she points to the photocopy machine.

At the start of April she collects the bar heaters from all the staff, to store them till next winter. When she comes for mine I plead, beg and cajole her to let me keep it. She giggles as she wrenches it forcibly from my hands then returns a few minutes later with the Thimphu telephone book. But of course.

Out of nowhere, the weather turns balmy. Looking up at Yeshe's *lhakhang* on the hill, I see spots of red: rhododendrons are blooming. Marijuana, too, flourishes in the warmth. It grows wild by the side of the freeway, in patches on our lawn and even bursts through a crack in the ground where I park the car. The sun at this altitude causes it to thrive. It has become a problem with some of the youth in town who smoke it, which is against the law, but mostly it is seen as a weed and fed to the pigs. Marijuana's active ingredient stores in the pig fat, which might explain why the Bhutanese like pork fat so much. When the weed overruns public spaces, Thimphu City Council burns it off, sending waves of heady smoke in all directions.

A cafe quietly opens in the street behind *Bhutan Observer*'s offices. It is not the first cafe in Thimphu, but it is the first with a real espresso machine, a trained barista and wireless internet. The owner, Karma, recently returned from two years in Australia. While his wife studied for her master's at the Australian National University, he waited tables at a Canberra cafe, learning the skills of a barista and how to run such a business. Karma's Coffee is the result. It serves excellent coffee, which appeals to foreigners working here as well as Bhutanese who have studied in countries with Starbucks. Customers meet or work on their laptops while Beyoncé shakes her booty on the flat-screen television hung on the wall.

When Karma opens his cafe, the advertising department invites him to advertise in *Bhutan Observer.* He laughs at the idea, saying the newspaper should pay him for the privilege of having his cafe in their pages. He is equally uninterested in co-operating with a reporter for a story on the About Town page, which features what is happening in Thimphu. He doesn't read newspapers and sees no reason to be in one – as a story or an advertisement.

The advertising department approaches another new cafe, this one offering a range of Western-style cakes, and the attitude is the same. *You should pay me if you want my business in your newspaper.*

Few Bhutanese businesses understand advertising. The government is responsible for 95 per cent of advertisements in the country's media. The other 5 per cent comes from a handful of the biggest businesses, such as Zimdra Automobiles and the hydropower companies. As I discovered with the *Faces of Bhutan* magazine, the rest of the business world only buys space when there is a royal occasion to commemorate, such as a coronation, an anniversary or the birthdays of the two Kings. The message is usually all about glory to His Majesty, and only occasionally do the companies actually mention their own businesses.

But Phuntsho also has principles about who should be allowed to advertise in the pages of her newspaper. *Bhutan Observer* doesn't carry advertisements for cars, because she feels that it would be unkind to make villagers desire something they can't afford. She has also turned down an astrologer from India who claimed he could repair broken marriages. 'That's not helpful to our society,' she says. She is emphatic: money or not, if it doesn't benefit society, it's not welcome in the pages of *Bhutan Observer.*

Coming from the mainstream Australian media, working for companies owned by Rupert Murdoch and Kerry Packer, I'm not used to this approach. In the Murdoch–Packer business model, advertising provides money for wages, publishing costs and profit – lots of profit. That might work on *Bhutan Times*, but it's clearly not Phuntsho's vision for *Bhutan Observer.* We are going to have to find alternative income streams to supplement the advertising income. And they are going to have to meet Phuntsho's formidable ethical code.

Phuntsho shows me a list of international 'days' she found on Wikipedia. The list runs to three pages. She has underlined ones relevant to Bhutan – World Malaria Day, Tuberculosis Day, Global Handwashing Day, International Day for Biological Diversity and more.

For World Malaria Day the Ministry of Health sponsors a colour lift-out explaining symptoms and how to treat them, as well as methods to stop mosquitoes breeding. It is informative, with photos of leaky pipes and marshy fields, all prime spots for mosquito breeding. It also features a message from the Health Minister and a photo of him looking dignified in his *gho* and orange shawl.

It is more like a school essay in its style and presentation than an eye-catching advertisement. But I appreciate that it would hit its target audience very successfully. Bhutan doesn't have billboards screaming catchphrases. There are no advertising flyers pasted to street signs or pushed through your letterbox. Companies don't shout slogans at you on the television. We are not bombarded with messages or information at every point of our day – life here is gloriously bereft of such noise. And with a lack of advertising comes a lack of cynicism: this World Malaria Day lift-out will be read as much as any other page of the newspaper.

Bhutan Observer uses this formula of sponsored lift-outs for public campaigns on World Tuberculosis Day, International Day for Biological Diversity and most of the other 'days' on Phuntsho's list. So do *Kuensel*, *Bhutan Times* and *Bhutan Today*. It would seem that every newspaper office has downloaded the list from Wikipedia.

The newspapers also target non-government organisations such as Danida (a Danish aid agency) and SNV (a Dutch aid agency). NGOs use advertising as a way to support the fledgling media industry and inject money into the community, while also communicating about an issue.

Phuntsho extends the sponsorship idea to a monthly supplement called *BO Focus*. It is an eight-page A5 booklet dedicated to a single issue such as the environment, food security or the importance of preserving Bhutanese culture. Here, Phuntsho provides a forum to pursue many of the topics that worry her. The newspaper approaches the relevant government department or NGO to sponsor it.

As well as providing income, the sponsored supplements are a perfect fit for her vision of a socially responsible newspaper, informing the Bhutanese and reinforcing Bhutanese values. But *Bhutan Observer* does not get enough of them to be financially sustainable.

Most of the government advertising in Bhutan is in the form of tenders. When the army plans to build a new wall in its barracks, it calls for tenders. When the Ministry of Health needs a photocopy machine, computer, tyres, or even stationery, it advertises its need in the newspaper. Businesses then submit a quote for their products or services. The style of advertising increases transparency, thereby helping prevent corruption.

The government places all its tenders in *Kuensel* and then alternates them between everybody else. As well as providing a financial advantage, this serves to entrench *Kuensel* as the newspaper that must be read. For a tyre distributor in Thimphu or a stationery shop, you only need *Kuensel* to see all the government tenders. Phuntsho and the management at *Bhutan Times* and *Bhutan Today* rail against this system, but change is slow. *Kuensel* is a government habit.

In an undeveloped economy like Bhutan's, government tenders are also stifling the growth of advertising for other businesses. Instead of businesses advertising to the customer, it is the customer who advertises to businesses. Money is not coming into the country from Xerox or Sony. The Bhutanese government is paying to advertise its needs to their representatives.

Furthermore, the predominance of government advertising makes the newspapers overly reliant on government favour, which ultimately can be dangerous. *Bhutan Observer* is fearless in its criticism of the government and specific ministries and departments. Phuntsho tells me the newspaper hasn't been refused advertisements as a reaction to publishing negative stories – yet. She expects it will happen and, as she has no intention of compromising the newspaper's editorial integrity, she dreads the day.

Opposition leader Tshering Tobgay says these fears are shared by *Bhutan Times*. Senior journalists have told him it is sometimes difficult to be critical of government because of the money.

'The advertisements and the felicitations come from the government. If you attack one office – Education, for instance – they feel Education will not be generous with them,' he says.

Tshering's advice to the journalists was not to write about their economic vulnerability, as it would only alert the government departments to the power they have. But he was ignored.

'I have said to the media, to senior journalists, don't ever tell people that you need the money that comes only from government advertisements and you are having difficulty because of that, and it somehow compromises your ability to write freely. Don't ever, ever write about it. But there have been editorials and opinions on that.'

In any case, this form of advertising cannot be relied on over the long term either. The government has announced its intention to put all its tenders online, once national broadband has been rolled out across the country. As always, *Bhutan Observer* needs to find other income streams.

Phuntsho hopes I might have some new ideas and asks me to work with the advertising department. Every Saturday I spend two hours with them, sipping tea in their sunny corner office and talking about the advertising end of the newspaper.

The team is made up of seven men and women in their early twenties, all bright-eyed and enthusiastic. Only Gopal, the department head, has studied marketing. The rest have come to the newspaper straight from school and figured out the job along the way.

Although I don't have an advertising background either, I have worked in newspapers and magazines enough to know a little about how it works. But I am also wary. I feel unclean, tainted. Phuntsho wants my Western experience but not my Western morality. I'm not offended: desire and consumerism *are* ugly, and I don't want to help them gain a foothold here. Advertorials, emotional manipulation, exaggeration, hype, dishonesty in any shape or form – those things are out. Benefiting all sentient beings is in.

Over a few weeks of discussion with the advertising department, a picture of the advertising business emerges, and we start to form a strategy. While people may buy *Bhutan Times* to cut out the photos of the latest Korean actor, readers buy *Bhutan Observer* for the stories. Our readers are educated and often important decision-makers – they are people from the affluent end of town, which ought to be attractive to advertisers. We come up with the line 'Trusted by the people you want to reach', and decide to create a media kit for potential advertisers.

We identify key sectors that we can target, such as banking and finance. Thimphu is also undergoing a building boom, with new shops and apartment blocks springing up everywhere. And with more than 80 per cent of the country involved in agriculture, we realise we need to find out more about what the Ministry of Agriculture is up to. What new programs are being trialled? How can we help?

In addition, we need to convince all the Karmas of Thimphu – the owners of new small businesses – of the benefits of advertising. To do so, we come up with a plan to offer Karma free advertising space to trial a discount voucher. We can then collect all the vouchers as proof that advertising works, to show other potential advertisers.

As the advertising pot is small in Bhutan, we also know we have to look outside the country. Many global products are sold here, particularly beauty brands, including Sunsilk and Garnier. Indian colleges also target potential Bhutanese students, and *Bhutan Observer*, which covers education better than the other newspapers, is well placed to take advantage of this. Bhutanese people also buy their house fittings from Indian towns across the border from Phuentsholing, so we will target the Indian companies to advertise in a lift-out building catalogue.

We divide up the jobs and each Saturday morning we report our progress. At first, everyone is fired up and I am buoyed by their enthusiasm. It does not last. One by one they droop back into the office. Thimphu City Corporation will not provide any figures on construction in case their figures are wrong. The Higher Education Association will not release information on Indian schools because it is none of our business. The Ministry of Agriculture will not tell us anything about their programs, not even allowing us to take a pamphlet, in case we publish the information.

I am dumbfounded. Each one of the advertising team is articulate, presentable and smart. What is going on here?

I complain to Phuntsho, saying I do not understand why these people refuse to do what is simply their job. 'These are government departments. This is public information. It should be available to anybody.'

She is amused by my indignation. 'They're Bhutanese. Everyone is scared of getting into trouble. Better not to do anything than to do something wrong.'

Still, I will not let the advertising team give up. We need that information. We role-play different arguments and they go back again and again. The staff are polite and charming, but determined. The excuses change, but not the outcome. 'Only my boss has those figures and he is out of station.' 'We can't find them.' 'They are out of date.'

While they endure knockback after knockback, I struggle to find a media agency that will represent the paper to international companies. One agency in Mumbai that does sound keen already represents *Kuensel*. When I ask about the conflict of interest, they say it would not matter – they have not got them any advertising in years. Hmm.

Nevertheless, we have some successes. The Ministry of Education suddenly provides a list of Indian schools accredited by the Bhutanese government. It turns out that the reason they wouldn't give it to us before is that they didn't have such a list. No-one had ever typed all the names onto one page. But they wouldn't say so directly.

The list is gold for us. These are the Indian colleges seeking Bhutanese students – a perfect fit for *Bhutan Observer*.

The director of Druk Holdings International, an umbrella organisation that liaises between government and businesses, comes in for a lively workshop with editorial and advertising. As a fan of the newspaper, he is thrilled to be invited and is full of news about which businesses are doing well, who to contact, all the gossip. After this meeting, Needrup plans a new economics page where the advertising department can sell space.

I work on the media kit with Gopal and graphic designer Sushil. We download a media kit from the *Indian Times* and model ours on that. We explain the strengths of *Bhutan Observer* and why Bhutan is a growing market, particularly for building and education. Tenzin has the kits printed in Delhi and they look great: small, vivid orange folders with the *Bhutan Observer* eye on the front, and fact sheets and a CD-ROM inside. When Phuntsho goes to a private hospital in Delhi for an eye operation, she hands one to her surgeon just before she goes under the anaesthetic. *Lots of potential patients in Bhutan*, she tells him. *Would you like to reach them?*

As for Karma, we explain how a voucher for his cafe would work, bringing him new customers and raising his profile. He is resolute – he will only agree if we pay him *and* reimburse him for the cost of every free coffee. He becomes a long-term challenge.

I am aware that my approach is all over the place and think the advertising department deserve proper training from someone who actually knows what they are doing. Phuntsho is supportive. What do I have in mind? I tell her about an old colleague in Australia, Katherine Rossetti, who has her own consultancy for business strategy and development. She has run sales teams for both major magazine companies in Australia, and has held senior positions in media agencies and digital media companies. For two years she ran a newspaper company in Vietnam, even launching a magazine there. Phuntsho can see the benefits of having Katherine's expertise and sets about convincing the government to fund her airfares.

I send Katherine an email. Would she leave her work and family, including her seven-year-old twins, to come to Bhutan to give some workshops, for no pay? Surprisingly, she says yes. Shangri-La appeals to just about everybody. Dolma prepares our spare bedroom for her arrival.

Katherine arrives with a suitcase full of marketing books, post-it notes and coloured textas. She hands them out in her first workshop then leads the advertising team through a series of questions, to build a profile and mental image of the *Bhutan Observer* reader.

> *How does he wake up?* With the sun.
> *What does he do first?* If he is religious, he will do his practice.
> *What would he have for breakfast?* A big traditional breakfast. Very big.
> *Get dressed in ...?* His *gho.*
> *Anything else?* Yes, a watch. But it wouldn't be a Rolex because the Fifth King doesn't have one of those. Diesel is a good brand. He would buy it in Bangkok. He would get into his car, a Prado, driven by his driver, to work, where he would have tea.
> *What would he take to a meeting? A briefcase?* No, a Parker pen.
> *Lunch?* He would go home for lunch with his wife or go out with other Dashos.
> *What is in his home?* He would have a house full of electronics – big plasma television, a washing machine, air conditioning if he lived in Phuentsholing.
> *Where would he go if he left the country?* He would take his family to Bangkok for holidays.

Katherine repeats it to me over lunch, saying she can see many potential advertising opportunities. I listen in during the afternoon session.

'Where's that place with Buddha? Where Buddha started?' she asks the team.

'Bodhgaya?' they suggest, referring to the spot in India where Buddha sat under the Bodhi Tree and attained enlightenment.

'Do Buddhists go there?' she asks.

The advertising department tell stories of people saving for years to send their parents on a pilgrimage to this sacred spot before they die. Every December, Druk Air puts on direct flights to Bodhgaya to cater for groups of Bhutanese pilgrims.

Katherine is thrilled. 'Okay, at the start of October we could do an advertising feature on Bodhgaya – where to stay, buses to get around … what else is on your Buddhist calendar?'

I marvel at how skilfully she applies her experience to the business at hand.

By the end of the week, post-it notes are plastered all over computers in the advertising department and the team is abuzz, their energy palpable. Katherine takes workshops each morning, and the rest of the time we utilise her vast experience in all areas of publishing.

I show her, with some pride, our media kit. She winces, saying she thinks we need something a bit sharper. The kit is filled with facts about the newspaper and the Bhutanese market, but Katherine explains that companies don't care what is good about *our* business. We have to talk about *their* business. Tell them what we can do for them. It sounds so obvious when she says it. She develops with the team a slick, targeted PowerPoint presentation and gives workshops on presenting.

Katherine is an expert in digital media, so she sits in on a management meeting to discuss IT. It turns out to be agony for both of us. The meeting is painfully slow. Phuntsho talks about hiring someone full-time to run IT for the newspaper and host the website forum. We go around the circle, giving our thoughts. Then we sit. Minutes pass with no-one speaking. Needrup adds a comment but falls silent again. After a couple of minutes he adds a further comment. Then we sit again. Not a word. Everyone looks at their feet except Katherine, whose eyes dart anxiously from person to person. I can feel her tension. She is not used to meetings where nothing happens. I feel her eyes on me and I wish I could say something to help. I can imagine her thoughts. *Have we finished? Is the meeting over?* Baffled, she says 'Right then,' in a tone of finality and goes to stand up, but everyone else stays seated.

I see myself in her agitation. I realise that this was me when I came here all those months ago. A model of efficiency, always with an eye on the next task. But the Bhutanese do not function that way. A meeting is not over till it's over. I realise how I have been tempered, diluted even. I can sit and wait now. Not doing anything. Just waiting till everyone has said what they would like to or Phuntsho feels the meeting is over, or we run out of tea. This glacial pace is probably the hardest thing for a Westerner to get used to. We don't do well with silence or inertia. Not socially, not in the office and certainly not in a meeting. If someone doesn't say something we tend to ignore them and move on. Busy, busy, busy.

In management meetings run by Phuntsho, if someone is quiet, she will gently draw them out. It is all about harmony, everyone having a say. Shared responsibility.

I feel like I am watching this from a great distance with recognition of both sides. I see the benefits and pitfalls of both. That efficiency, that drive for productivity, is often criticised for being stressful. Perhaps. But it also means things get done. Phuntsho could do with a bit more of it in her office.

But there is also something friendly and companionable about sitting in silence with work colleagues. No pressure to speak. No haste. Everything in good time. I have come to like it, a lot.

Phuntsho declares Katherine's three-week visit a success. It has given her new ideas and long-term plans for her company. The advertising team are also grateful, and show their appreciation by taking Katherine for a traditional Bhutanese picnic. They hire a minibus to go to a neighbouring valley and all get roaring drunk on Bhutanese whisky, before dropping her home in the early hours of the morning, falling over each other as they deliver her to our front door, all promising lifelong friendship via Facebook.

But it is after she has gone that the effects of her short visit are really noticeable. The advertising team is confident and enthused. I see them leaving the office looking polished in their *ghos* and *kiras*, each with an office laptop under their arm, ready to take their new slick PowerPoint presentation out into the Thimphu business world. Eat your heart out, *Kuensel*.

21

The Outside World

When you're living in Bhutan, it can be easy to forget the rest of the world exists. But often the outside world comes to Thimphu. Celebrities visit to revel in the anonymity. And politicians come too, though their reasons for doing so are less clear. A month after John McCain's loss to Barack Obama, he arrives in Bhutan with a 15-member delegation. His photograph with the Fifth King appears on the front page of *Bhutan Observer.* Representatives from governments in Kuwait, India, Denmark and Australia visit over a three-month period. On 18 May it is Israel's turn.

Months after Operation Cast Lead, the horrific 22-day attack on Gaza, which ended in January 2009, Israeli diplomats launch a charm offensive across the world. Having been roundly criticised for the bloodbath that killed about 1,400 Palestinians and 13 Israelis, the country sets about reworking their image on the international stage. On the same day Israeli Prime Minister Benjamin Netanyahu meets with Barack Obama in the White House, his India-based representative arrives in Thimphu. Eli Belotsercovsky is Deputy Chief of Mission at the Israeli embassy in New Delhi. As part of a three-day goodwill visit, he has requested a meeting with *Bhutan Observer.*

Phuntsho, Tenzin, Needrup and I receive him in the boardroom. I know Phuntsho is impressed by the diplomatic status of our visitor because she has the office maid bring out the porcelain cups with lids for tea.

Eli is a tall, long-faced man in a dark grey suit, who reminds me faintly of an old boyfriend. Except Eli does not smile. At all. He asks polite questions that Phuntsho, Tenzin and Needrup answer as best they can. I guess from Eli's face that he is having trouble processing their responses.

Israel has no diplomatic, historical or cultural ties with Bhutan and, as far as I can tell, the two countries have little in common. But Eli does not let that stand in the way of a new friendship. He is here to win over the newspaper and he throws himself in. He says Israel is keen to strengthen relationships and wants to help Bhutan. He knows the two countries are very different and that his own country has 'some troubles' but he is here to offer help.

The Bhutanese are used to countries throwing money at them. The Japanese paid for garbage trucks; Australia sent firemen and sheep; Denmark funded a bodyguard business; Switzerland developed potato farming; Austria donated millions towards 'good governance'; and so on. At one stage a consortium of European countries donated expensive mill machinery to enable the Bhutanese to earn an income from their forests. Some years later, Scandinavian countries donated millions to close down the business, compensate the workers and save the trees.

The Bhutanese accept such international generosity as their due. They believe the wisdom of their Kings has given the country good karma. The fact that Israel wants to help does not seem unusual. When Eli makes his offer, I can see Phuntsho's mind working furiously. Where to start? There are so many areas where the newspaper needs help. Denmark funded *Kuensel*'s webpage, but *Bhutan Observer* already has one of those. She and Tenzin would like to build their own printing press, but they also need more office space, new computers, experienced staff … She starts with the staff.

Eli responds that in Israel they have many newspapers, so he is sure they can help train reporters, but then he edges the conversation back to Israel itself. He wants to understand the newspaper's views on his country. He does not mention the 22-day conflict in Gaza, which was not covered by the Bhutanese media. I saw it on CNN, along with Netanyahu arriving at the White House, so I think I know what it is he is trying to say. But he speaks in such vague terms that the Bhutanese haven't a clue. What do they think of his country? They look confused, so he changes tack. What international newspapers do they have a relationship with?

Most newspapers have publishing arrangements with foreign newspapers, giving them access to news from overseas without having to fund their own reporters on the ground. Once Eli knows which international newspapers *Bhutan Observer* buys stories from, he can get some idea of its political views and how it might be reporting Israel.

'We sometimes send interns to India to do internships at the newspapers,' Needrup responds helpfully.

I feel empathy for Eli, as I remember how I struggled to get my head around Phuntsho's very specific vision for her newspaper. I try to help, and explain they don't have relationships with anybody. *Bhutan Observer* doesn't report international news. They don't take news feeds from anywhere, including agencies such as Reuters or Associated Press. Eli looks at me in disbelief and it is all I can do not to laugh. I realise how I no longer find that odd. Sitting in this boardroom on the top of the world, with the sounds of discordant trumpets wafting in from a *puja*, it makes sense. I try to explain that some newspapers here reprint a couple of stories off the internet but *Bhutan Observer* decided not to. They believe that Bhutanese who are interested in the wider world can watch it on CNN and BBC.

'What about news analysis? The global financial crisis?' asks Eli.

Needrup explains that for something like the world recession they would invite their best Bhutanese scholars to comment.

Eli asks about science and technology. No one responds.

Eli continues: '*The Times of India* have a full page. I realise *Bhutan Observer* is not in that category yet but how do you report on science and technology?'

Needrup shakes his head and Phuntsho explains they don't. This is a *truly* Bhutanese model for a newspaper, she declares. Her tone makes it clear that she is proud that Bhutanese people want to read about what happens *inside* the country. I watch as the realisation dawns on Eli's face.

'You report only on what happens *inside* Bhutan?' He looks both incredulous and shocked. 'You report no international news … at all?'

They nod proudly. Eli is at a loss for words. He opens his mouth and then closes it again. There really is nothing left to say, and he stands to leave.

His Bhutanese driver takes him off for the rest of his tour, including a visit to the Gross National Happiness Commission, which has the final say on all government policies – any policy that doesn't make society a happier place, regardless of its economic benefits, will not be approved. I wish I could go with him. I cannot begin to imagine what that meeting will be like.

Eli's visit is a reminder that outside the country the world is a troubled place, facing massive challenges. Mal and I keep up with international news on CNN, BBC and online news sites, and are well aware of the global financial crisis that has captured the world's attention. But the crisis has mostly passed Bhutan by. The country is so cut off from the world economy that it will have little effect. The two Bhutanese banks are not part of the international banking system. Visa, MasterCard and American Express cannot be used here. The ngultrum is pegged to the Indian rupee but remains worthless outside the country. Even though the rupee is accepted in Bhutanese shops, banks on the Indian side of the border will not exchange ngultrum.

Bhutan exports agriculture, hydropower and cement to India, but most of the country's income comes as an annual donation from India. Due to Bhutan's strategic location – wedged between India and China – India considers supporting Bhutan an important part of their own national security and will continue to do so, regardless of the global financial crisis. It behaves in many ways like a protective big brother to Bhutan, training its army, providing the services of its own air force and maintaining an army presence within the country. Bhutan and India have a friendly arrangement where their citizens can work and travel in both countries without requiring a visa or passport. In matters of its own government and foreign relations, however, Bhutan maintains its independence.

As the leader of the world's newest democracy, Prime Minister Thinley was invited to address the United Nations. He took the opportunity to suggest a Bhutanese approach to the financial crisis:

> We need to wake up from our narcissistic slumber and self-indulgence, and realise that economic wellbeing is not human wellbeing. We must break away from the shackles of the powerful forces of the market. For that matter, could the unravelling of the market-based economy, as evident in the financial crisis, be a glimpse of the truth that mindless and irresponsible economic growth cannot go on. It is neither sustainable nor fair to future generations. Above all, we could be condemning our own selves to an old age of burdensome debt and regret?
>
> This brings us to the question, are our fundamentals sound? Is the GDP-led growth that has served as our measure of progress good enough for the future? What are the foundations of our civilisation and the values that guide us? As we get richer and live by the terms that we have set for ourselves, are we truly becoming more civilised

> or is it a downward spiral of de-civilisation in which we are trapped? Does economic growth translate as human development? Are we mutating to become senseless robots programmed to be materially productive, to earn more, to want more, to consume more and more of what we do not need and will ultimately destroy us?
>
> As human beings, should we not search for and be driven by higher values? Do we not have needs beyond the material, beyond that of the body alone? Can we conceptualise a holistic alternative paradigm for meaningful and sustainable development that places the wellbeing of the individual and community at the centre and gives cause for true happiness as opposed to fleeting pleasures?

This historic event was a moment of satisfaction and triumph for the Bhutanese, who are proud that their attitudes to money and economic growth differ from those of other countries. *Bhutan Times* reported the Prime Minister's speech on its front page, praising his elegance and humility – 'the small Bhutan flag pinned to his simple black *gho*'. *Kuensel* published an editorial six days later, describing the speech as offering a 'Himalayan perspective' on the Wall Street crisis.

The rest of the world press, however, ignored the speech – and advice – completely. Outside Bhutan it was not reported. The Prime Minister's voice was drowned out by the cacophony of the world media trying to understand how the global financial crisis happened and who was to blame.

Bhutan's media also did not dwell on it for long. Very quickly, journalists moved back to more immediate concerns – the potato harvest, a *lhakhang* robbery, the Fifth King's forthcoming visit to the east. The only references in newspapers to the global financial crisis are comments from the government that tourism may be down in the coming year. The crisis that sends shock waves around the world, directly affecting billions, and becoming one of the defining news stories of the decade, is just not of interest to the majority of Bhutanese.

22

Floods of Change

On the morning of 26 May 2009, Mal, Kathryn and I cross the little bridge from Tashi Pelkhil village and drive straight into Bhutan's biggest traffic jam. We squeeze into a line of three rickety old buses, each overflowing with monks. The traffic is moving so slowly that boy monks get out and run back and forth between them. Their heads are freshly shaved and they are grinning. Robes flying, sandals flapping. Thousands of cheering well-wishers line the road, ignoring the drizzling rain. We wonder what we have missed – what's the celebration? Did Bhutan win an archery tournament?

We have become used to not knowing what is going on around us. Public announcements about road closures and the like are often only in the Dzongkha edition of BBS evening news. Somehow word of mouth means every Bhutanese person keeps up, but no-one thinks to mention it to us *chillips*.

Mal leans out and asks a monk trotting beside our car what is going on. 'It is the first day of the fourth month of our calendar,' he explains. 'We are back!'

It is the monk body returning to Thimphu from their winter retreat. This means the worst of the cold weather really is over.

I understand the exuberance, and feel like hugging the monks.

It takes us an hour of weaving through traffic to get to the office. It takes His Holiness the Je Khenpo much longer. He is mobbed every inch of the way by people seeking his blessing. Opposition leader Tshering Tobgay writes in his blog that it takes almost seven hours for the Je Khenpo to drive the seven kilometres from one side of Thimphu to his home at Tashichhodzong on the other.

It rains for the rest of the day, a sign that the south-west monsoon is coming early. From my office I can see Yeshe's *lhakhang* and the BBS tower poking through a ring of cloud. It looks impossibly eerie. I watch the cloud slide noiselessly down the slope until we are engulfed in dense, silvery fog. I can just make out Rita's toilet block opposite the newspaper building.

No one wants to leave the comfort of the office, but the relentless rain has moved from minor annoyance to major news story. We can see the roads beginning to flood. Needrup sends out the staff photographer, who brings back evocative photos showing the Wang Chhu river as a bubbling, seething mass carrying debris and even cars. We all stare at them on the screen in the newsroom. Needrup looks pained. It is only Tuesday and the next edition of *Bhutan Observer* doesn't go out till Friday.

Kuensel, which went from bi-weekly to six editions a week a month ago, are bound to publish their photos tomorrow, as will the daily newspaper, *Bhutan Today*.

Needrup decides to post our photos on the *Bhutan Observer* website. It is the first time I have seen him do that. As it only attracts a handful of visitors each day, updating the *Bhutan Observer* site is not a priority. But this is major breaking news, and Needrup is a newsman.

BBS starts broadcasting footage of people wading through waist-high water with furniture on their heads and police evacuating homes near the Queen Grandmother's palace. They put it all together on a continuous loop. It is effective the first time I see it, giving a sense of the scale of the flooding and how people across Thimphu are being affected. But it is not much help after that. BBS does not update the footage or provide advice for residents, with no reporting of the rain or flooding as news. It is that same ten minutes of silent footage, again and again. As the only Bhutanese television station, it is painfully inadequate.

A woman rings Needrup and tells him *Bhutan Observer* must report that the Prime Minister is the reason for the rain. He is a bad spirit. She warns that the rain will only stop if the previous prime minister is reinstated. Needrup, ever polite, thanks her for ringing.

A journalist reports back that the newly opened Centenary Farmers Market, Thimphu's architectural pride and joy, is awash with mud. Clogged sewage pipes have given way, spilling their contents onto footpaths and roads.

The Home Minister faxes a statement to the newspapers and BBS radio, telling people not to travel or go to the riverbanks to watch the flood. As most people have a mobile phone and streaming radio is popular, it should be an effective way to spread a public service message. Instead, it seems to inspire residents to see what all the fuss is about. By the time Mal and Kathryn collect me from work, crowds are lining the banks for kilometres, some wading into the murky water to grab pieces of wood as they float past. Others wade in to catch fish, which are suffocating in the muddy waters and floating to the surface. There are traffic jams as drivers abandon their cars on the expressway to check out the spectacle. The atmosphere is like that of a street party.

Wang Chhu is an extraordinary sight. Usually the river is an arctic green, the water fast-flowing but clear enough to see white rocks on the bottom. Today it is brown and bubbling like a chocolate milkshake, steadily rising up the banks, uprooting trees along the way. The sound is an all-pervading roar, as if we are standing on an airport runway.

When we reach our little bridge back to Tashi Pelkhil, Mal pulls over to check its foundations. The smell of dirt fills the air. It is earthy and wet and rather lovely. Tonnes of topsoil, dead fish and whole trees thunder past under our feet, heading for India. Mal says the bridge looks safe enough and shows me where its fault lines are. If the foundations are undermined, this is where cracks will appear. He traces an imaginary line with his foot and tells me if I see a mark here, I am not to cross. This is supposed to make me feel safe.

It rains all night and for the next two days. Tshering Tobgay uploads footage of the swollen river to YouTube and then embeds it on his blog. His excitement is palpable. He writes that he has been practising uploading videos but this is a first for his blog, which he started six months ago. It is also a first for Bhutan. News footage online. Tshering Tobgay, whose blog averages about 300 hits a day, is leading the way. For those with access to the internet, the Opposition leader is forging a formidable reputation as a one-man news outlet. He updates it every evening on his laptop, sitting up in bed. Sometimes he comments on government matters; other times he reports on what is going on in the communities he visits.

Flooding takes out bridges and homes, and causes landslides that block the national highway. The death toll reaches nine – six farmers, a road worker and two children. One of them, a seven-year-old schoolboy, drowns a few hundred metres downriver from our home. He loses his footing trying to cross on his way home from school. When the rain finally stops and the sun does reappear, the city is devastated.

But worse is to come. Just two months later, on 27 July, when the monsoon has well and truly arrived across Bhutan, the country faces a national tragedy.

In Chhukha, south-east Bhutan, seven schoolboys drown in the most heartbreaking circumstances. They are all students at the lower elementary school, in a town of fewer than 3,000 people. The boys, aged 10 to 18, lie to their parents that they are going to spend Sunday studying at school. It is the height of summer, and they sneak off with their lunchboxes and meet at a popular swimming hole on the river. They wade through the knee-deep water, leaping across rocks, and reach the opposite bank. They dive into the river and splash about together, having fun. At lunchtime they light a fire for their picnic, when suddenly the river starts to rise and they are blocked from going back the way they came. It starts to rain heavily and the boys begin to panic. They make it across the river to a large rock in the middle, but are too scared to go further. The eldest, Tshering Samten, feels responsible for the younger ones and tries to swim to another rock. He is swept away but makes it to the bank 100 metres downstream. He yells to the boys to stay where they are and goes for help. The village is over an hour away, mostly uphill through jungle. He gets lost, and it is dark when he reaches his parents. They inform the mayor, who puts together an ad-hoc rescue team comprising ten police officers, ten army officers, 21 village officials and five parents. They all race to the river, arriving at about 10 pm. There, they find the seven terrified boys huddled together, chanting prayers on a rock in the middle of the raging water. For the next five or six hours, by flickering torchlight, the adults try to rescue them. They throw nylon ropes, but over the noise of the raging water, the boys cannot understand instructions. There is massive confusion in the darkness, with dwindling torch batteries, dense fog, howling wind and constant rain. The boys tie the ropes around themselves, tethering the seven of them together. Around 3 am a sudden gush of water sweeps down the river. The series of ropes that is tied around all the boys, and held at the other end by parents and villagers, comes undone. The parents watch in horror as their children are swept away. Some race downriver and throw themselves into the water to try to catch the boys, but they are impotent against the torrent.

The country is left reeling. It is not the first time Bhutan has suffered a national tragedy, but it is the first time they have had such an open and public space to collectively express their grief. Before democracy there was only *Kuensel*. It would have reported the facts, expressed the condolences of the government and King, and perhaps written an editorial to give the tragedy some sort of philosophical context. I imagine BBS would have reported it in their news service.

But now there are also three independent newspapers, each with reporters, editors, columnists and letters pages. And there are blogs – the Opposition leader's, and others. There is Facebook.

And most significantly, the Bhutanese have started to find their voice. Since the Fourth King announced the move to democracy, the people have been encouraged to pay attention, have an opinion and express it. It is part of their responsibilities as citizens in this new democracy. Emboldened, many throw themselves into the new, expanding public space created by the new, modern media.

At first, there is a massive outpouring of grief and pain, which reverberates throughout Bhutan in an unprecedented manner. The expanded public space amplifies people's emotions. And it happens at a bewildering speed.

In the first two days the newspapers publish stories explaining what happened, without blame or sensationalism. They are often contradictory, reflecting the confusion of the night. The editorials are thoughtful and measured. *Kuensel* writes that accidents have happened before and will happen again, adding philosophically: 'Fatalism is an integral part of our psyche, shaped by the belief that our destiny has already been charted by how we lived our previous lives.'

But very quickly a seam of anger and resentment rises to the surface, first appearing in columns and letters and blogs. The Bhutanese cannot accept that police, army and government officials struggled for six hours and still the boys died. In chat rooms, citizens make inflammatory, sometimes nasty comments, while hiding behind anonymity.

The Bhutanese want to yell at someone; they just cannot agree who. Older rural people believe that the deaths were caused by wrathful river deities. In Thimphu and larger cities, some blame the government or the police, while others question if any role was played by the Chhukha hydropower station, which is a few kilometres upriver from the site of the tragedy. Questions are asked on blogs, in letters and editorials, as well as in homes and offices across Thimphu. *Why weren't police able to rescue the children? What about the senior officials? What were they doing in those six hours? Why was there no warning from upstream? Whenever a Westerner is hurt in the mountains, they are choppered out. Why didn't the government send a helicopter for Bhutanese children? Are their lives worth less?*

Needrup sums up the mood of the nation in his Friday editorial:

> Early this week, seven boys died after staring death in the face for hours. For the nation, the initial reaction was shock. As the details of the failed rescue operation emerged and everybody mulled over the tragedy, the shock gave way to regret, pity and helplessness. Now the national sentiment carries an undertone of anger and frustration. In hindsight, every other person on the street thinks that the boys could have been rescued.

On the day Needrup's editorial is published, the anger and frustration he writes about reaches a crescendo and spills from the newspapers and cyberspace onto the street. As the morning unfolds, many Thimphu residents come to the sacred *chorten*, a type of Bhutanese shrine, near the centre of town, to light butter lamps in the traditional way of Bhutanese mourning. One thousand are lit. But then a group of Thimphu citizens do something entirely un-Bhutanese. Around 100 'march' from the *chorten* to the swimming pool, about 300 metres away. Watched by police and one or two curious onlookers, they walk in silence behind a large poster showing a photo of flickering butter lamps and the words 'In Memoriam; remembering the seven young lives lost in Chhukha'.

The idea for the march originated in the offices of *Bhutan Times*, then spread to other newspapers and beyond. The marchers are mostly people from the media, with some civil servants. At the swimming pool they hand over a petition addressed to the Prime Minister. It reads, in part:

> We cannot help but feel the duty of the citizenry to seize the opportunity to build a collective national consciousness and to let the nation know that we have come together, to awaken ourselves and take action, and to seek explanation for this tragedy, so that seven lives, albeit irredeemable, have not been lost in vain; so that the turmoil felt by the six stricken families is assuaged; so that the doubts, questions and emotions of sorrow and anger, which the nation is justifiably feeling, are appropriately addressed.
>
> Concerned Citizens of Bhutan

The marchers are not aggressive or threatening. Rather, they seem earnest and subdued. Most of them are in their twenties, a few in their thirties, and all are neatly dressed in *ghos* and *kiras*. They look enthused, engaged and, to my eye, somehow healthy and wholesome. *Bhutan Today* reports the next day that the people 'exercised their right to peaceful assembly as granted by article 7.12 of the Constitution of Bhutan'. To me it looks like democracy, in all its aspects, is flourishing.

But I am wrong.

If the country was shocked by the boys' deaths, it is nothing to their reaction to Bhutanese 'demonstrating' on the streets of Thimphu.

Many see the march as the beginning of the end. Total anarchy. Next it will be rabid crowds setting fire to trucks, just like their neighbours in India and Nepal.

A few of the *Bhutan Observer* staff took part, but Phuntsho disapproves. She cringes at turning grief into a public spectacle. She says it is un-Bhutanese. It would have been more effective if they had lit lamps. She lit butter lamps in her shrine room at home, quietly, on her own, and said prayers for the boys and their families.

The tragedy of the boys' deaths is momentarily replaced in the media by news about the march. The motivation of the marchers varies: some call it a solidarity march, others a peace walk, and still others say it is a strike. Some say they want to show the grieving parents that all of Bhutan grieves with them. Some blame the government that they could not save those children.

At a dinner a few nights later, held by the Vice Chancellor of the Royal University of Bhutan, the march dominates the conversation. Among the handful of Westerners present, none seems to think the march was a big deal. Even using the term 'march' seems at odds with what we saw. But the 40 or so Bhutanese see it very differently. Not one of them is supportive.

The newspapers also come under fire, in particular *Bhutan Times* for its gratuitous coverage of the grieving families. Their reporter goes back again and again to interview the 18-year-old boy who made it to safety and sounded the alarm. One story is headlined 'Their screams still haunt me'.

But according to the people present at the Vice Chancellor's dinner, the newspaper has reached a new low that morning with its front page, which carries a photo of a row of empty children's chairs. Beneath are photos of six of the boys. The seventh box has no picture and carries the words 'Tashi Penjor did not even leave a photograph behind'. It is excruciatingly maudlin.

The story is not unlike many that fill tabloid newspapers in the

English-speaking world after a catastrophe. But that does not make it welcome in Bhutan. Again, *Bhutan Times* has crossed a line they did not know existed.

'That was the final straw,' says Kunzang Choden, the outspoken international writer. 'Emotive. Playing on heartstrings. We don't want that kind of reporting in Bhutan.'

The Vice Chancellor's wife feels for the grieving families who are living through this media maelstrom. 'If I was one of the parents, I would be devastated to read all this. Leave the families alone,' she says.

The *Bhutan Times* approach is certainly very tabloid, and the way the Bhutanese at the dinner responded would suggest that is not appreciated here. They recoil against such overt emotional manipulation.

Literacy levels are low and those who can read do not necessarily read newspapers. Only the educated elite voluntarily read newspapers and engage in public discussion. There is no populist readership, which in the West has traditionally been the market for tabloid-style news. *Bhutan Today* publishes Hollywood or Bollywood celebrity photographs, but they are not particularly salacious. The occasional appearance of Jennifer Aniston in the paper is really an excuse to run her photo. The accompanying story, if there is one, usually reports briefly on a new movie, not speculation on her love life. Nor is there tabloid-style television. There is an innocence, a lack of hype, in the public space opening up in Bhutan. It would seem that its educated citizens are demanding this space be treated with seriousness and integrity.

The Bhutanese present at the Vice Chancellor's dinner are equally unhappy about the march itself. As head of the Bhutan Centre for Media and Democracy, Siok Sian Pek-Dorji is uncomfortable that most of the marchers were journalists. It is not their role to be activists, she says.

A senior civil servant says newspapers are there to report news, not make it.

Kunzang Choden questions the motivation of the marchers. As with Phuntsho, it is the public nature of the gesture that makes her cringe. She tells me that they are stealing someone else's grief for their own purpose. It won't help the families. 'It would mean more if they went to the temple,' she says.

For weeks, the march – and the anarchy it could presage – continues to be big news. It is dissected and debated on blogs and in the newspapers. Popular blog *www.kuzuzangpo.com* publishes a range of views.

'Years from now, the death of the 7 unfortunate children will be remembered as an event that ushered in a movement that gave birth to the social evil known as STRIKES,' writes 'The Laggard'.

'I for one don't see anything wrong with the "Solidarity Walk" … strikes and protests are some of the major tools in democratic set up; of course it has to be in the interest of the larger mass,' responded '123'.

After a few days, news that the Fourth King disapproves of the march filters through Thimphu society, which confirms what the majority seems to be feeling.

The government announces an inquiry into the deaths of the seven boys. When it comes out, four months later, it covers everything raised by the Solidarity March petition. Ultimately, everyone is absolved from responsibility. Nothing more could have been done for the boys. Everyone involved saves face, and when the report is presented to parliament, there is barely a murmur in response. The newspapers report the findings and quickly move on.

I don't think anyone in Bhutan would consider the nation's first public march to have been a success. It scared them, bringing the violent unrest that seems part of civic life in Nepal and India a little too close. With democracy comes new freedom, as well as power. The Bhutanese are testing this power and discovering its limits. This can mean going further than what they are comfortable with. And while the general public is figuring out the new parameters, so is the government and so is the media.

23

Getting Along with Elephants

In August the weather is moist and hot, and the land is fertile. The marijuana growing wild by the side of the road is taller than me and the sunflowers at Tashi Pelkhil are like bouncing smiley faces, nodding as we pass. The trees are heavy with apples and pears. Mal buys avocados at the market that are the size of small cantaloupes.

I feel a different sense of time. Everything feels like a long time ago, even when it was only yesterday. Time has stretched or bent or something. It is hard to put my finger on. I just know it is different. Philosopher Blaise Pascal famously said that all of humanity's problems stem from man's inability to sit quietly in a room alone. I find I am getting better at it and it is having an effect, which is inexplicable and rather lovely.

As our departure date approaches, we start our farewells, which in Bhutan are a protracted affair. It feels like everybody we have ever met invites us for dinner or a picnic or appears in my office with a farewell gift. Our landlords, Kinley and Choeden, invite us for dinner, which means walking across our driveway to their home next door. Kinley, who is handsome and 40-ish, has lived at Tashi Pelkhil village since he was seven and entertains us with stories of an idyllic childhood with his siblings, before roads or electricity. He tells of riding his horse down to the river and wading through rice paddies where our home now stands. But, he says, if we think Tashi Pelkhil has changed now, we will not recognise it in another year.

We have been noticing the building works going on in the barren wasteland over our fence, and heard through the maid network that the Goenling family was doing something big. But no-one has prepared us for just how big. Kinley explains that the General's children are building an exclusive international-standard high school at Tashi Pelkhil, complete with football fields and a Japanese judo room. One sister plans to build an apartment block next to her home, to rent out to school families. The little bridge covered in prayer flags will not cope with all the new traffic, so the brothers will build a new, larger one to take cars and pedestrians directly from the expressway into a car park. They would like to build a hotel in the orchard. The high school will open in six months, and next week they will start advertising in *Kuensel* for teachers and a principal.

Mal and I are stunned. Our multicultural enclave, so sleepy and safe, will soon be abuzz with activity. We feel sad that the serene little village will be lost but have to admire their bravado. None of the family has any experience as teachers or in the education department, and yet they are starting a school. Phuntsho and Tenzin had no experience in the media, and they started a newspaper. This spirit of entrepreneurship is in the air. This is the time for Bhutanese who have ideas and the courage to have a go. The middle class is growing and so are the opportunities.

But the General's family is not building a school just because it makes good business sense. Kinley and Choeden tell us they were sent to boarding school in India from a young age – Kinley at five and Choeden at six. Neither enjoyed the experience, feeling lonely and missing their families. They want to create a better experience for the next generation. Their vision is to provide world-class facilities so that parents who prefer a private education, and can afford it, do not have to send their children to board in Indian schools.

Kinley says the new school will try to pass on to students the values that the General has exemplified throughout his life. They have come up with a motto for the school: *Veritas, humilitas, integritas.* Truth, humility, integrity.

An American couple, posted here by the World Bank, will take over our lease the minute we leave. Our Dutch, Danish and Uzbekistani neighbours are also moving on over the next few months to new exotic posts, with new foreigners lining up to take over their leases. I feel how life constantly changes, everything shifting around, nothing standing still for a moment.

In the office I hear about yet another newspaper that is set to launch, this time aimed at the business community and owned by two Thimphu women – a successful businesswoman and a wealthy housewife. They start trying to poach journalists. *Bhutan Today* loses a few and so does *Bhutan Times.* Needrup and Rabi are both offered higher salaries but decline, saying their heart is with *Bhutan Observer.*

We start shedding belongings to fly home, and Mal presents his coffee machine to our neighbour Megan. The maids of Tashi Pelkhil are delighted and immediately embrace cafe culture, gathering at her home for their morning break, requesting their various preferences – latte, flat white, espresso.

The newspaper staff farewell us with a traditional Bhutanese picnic in a park outside Thimphu. Rows of hot dishes are lined up. Everyone, it seems, has brought their own family version of the national dish, *ema datshi,* made with chilli and cheese. We sample them all, tears streaming down our faces, agreeing that each one really is the best. Then Needrup makes a lovely speech, saying impossibly nice things, and we all get very drunk on Bhutanese whisky.

The maids of Tashi Pelkhil take us for a picnic at another park and Dolma gets teary, which makes me teary, which embarrasses our daughters completely. Dolma's husband, in a sober moment, sends us a card thanking us for looking after his family.

We spend our final night at a dinner in our honour at the home of Phuntsho and Tenzin. Their living room is also the shrine room, where Phuntsho says her prayers every morning, aspiring to benefit all sentient beings that day. One wall is covered in gold statues of Buddha, Guru Rinpoche and various Buddhist deities. She lights butter lamps, bathing them all in a warm glow.

She presents us with a magnificent handmade rug, from the best carpet weaver in Bhutan, made to her own specifications. It is deep blue, featuring two golden dragons, the symbol of Bhutan, holding a large jewel that represents Buddha's teachings. Then she hands us a small bundle, wrapped in cotton wool. It is an exquisite brass statue of Tara, the feminine aspect of Buddha. We feel utterly humbled and I kick myself for not bringing gifts. No-one else seems at all concerned.

Phuntsho has managed to source riverweed and wild ferns, both rare delicacies, and prepared them just as her grandmother does, back in the village. We toast the newspaper, Needrup's editorship and each other.

After sharing their daily worries and aspirations for the newspaper, it feels surreal to say goodbye, to just walk away. We promise to keep in touch by email, aware that we may never see each other again. We share brief hugs at the doorstep, then we are off into the night, feeling sad but also buoyant. The adventure is over, but it was a good one and now home is calling.

The next morning, as the sun is rising, Phuntsho and Tenzin appear out of the mist with hot, sweet tea in a flask and steaming chapattis wrapped in tea towels. They want to share one last meal together before we leave for the airport.

*

If saying goodbye was difficult, it is nothing compared to re-assimilating into our own culture. For the first few weeks back home in Sydney's inner west, we are like rabbits in the headlights. Stricken. Mal ventures out to buy food and loses half a day at the local shopping mall, stuck in the muesli aisle, paralysed by choice. He rings to ask what sort he should get – gluten-free, extra grains, brown grain, with apricot … I tell him I have no idea. I am still sitting in the same spot at home where he left me. I haven't got past the first page of the newspaper. It is packed with words and pictures and information. I read every photo caption, every advertisement, every single word on the page. I seem to have lost the ability to skim or discern. Brochures yelling at us to buy, buy, buy pour into our letterbox, get pushed under the door and fall out of the newspaper, piling up on surfaces around the house, demanding attention. It is a cacophony and I feel under siege. Kathryn and I unpack a box of belongings and she sits on the floor – surrounded by books, toys and clothes – looking dazed. 'So much stuff,' she says, and pushes it away. I know how she feels.

I remember a Melbourne couple, the Claypoles, who in the mid 1990s spent a year in a hut on the ice at Antarctica. When they returned to their four-bedroom home in the Melbourne suburbs, they were unable to unpack the boxes they had so carefully stored. The contents, they said, now seemed irrelevant. I understand how they felt.

Kathryn adjusts quickly, happy to be back with her schoolfriends. They ask her how Bhutan was, she says 'good', and that's the end of it. She seamlessly slips back into their interests. Mal and I take much longer. We do everything we can *not* to leave the house. Everyone talks too loud, too fast, and stands too close. I have trouble following the pace of conversation. I meet two friends for coffee and cannot keep up as they leap from topic to topic. I feel like the dull country cousin – slow and dense.

I am repulsed by the consumerism that pervades our life in Australia. It is obscene. New-season fashions, new looks for your home, update your car. Whatever for? It all seems so utterly pointless. And shameful. But it is the conversation that dominates our public space. I had never noticed how much the noise of commerce blocks out everything else. I can't get through a half-hour show on commercial television – the advertisements are an assault on the senses. And the politics is brutal, ugly. Everyone seems so rude.

Gradually we adjust. We rediscover our filters. The billboard posters and bus advertisements start to recede into the background hum. The glossy brochures go straight from the letterbox and the newspaper into the recycling bin, without requiring any attention along the way. I relearn how to read our daily newspaper, skimming and scanning with abandon. People's conversations start to come into focus and we re-engage with friends, family and what's happening in this part of the world. It takes a few months but eventually life returns to full warp speed, the pace of modern Australian life.

But there is a part of me that doesn't catch up – a little corner of my being that cannot share the excitement of having the biggest IKEA in the southern hemisphere open a few suburbs away. I hanker for the slower pace of Bhutan, with its gentler, kinder society, which constantly asks itself, *Will this make us happier? Is this benefiting* all *our community?*

Phuntsho puts me on the *Bhutan Observer* subscription list, and each Friday a PDF of the newspaper arrives in my inbox. It lands midmorning, after I've read our own newspaper. Through Needrup's editorials I can follow what's worrying Thimphu, 9,400 kilometres away, while keeping up with all Bhutan's news – from the King granting *kidu*, to the government helping farmers make friends with pesky elephants that keep trampling their crops in the middle of the night. It's like a little portal into the parallel universe that is Druk Yul, land of the thunder dragon:

First elephant awareness workshop
by Eshori Gurung

Elephants and humans are in constant conflict in southern Bhutan. To ease this tension and create awareness among the stakeholders, the Nature Conservation Division under Ministry of Agriculture and Forests is organising the first human–elephant co-existence workshop in Lobesa, Wangdue. The workshop started yesterday.

Titled 'Getting Along with Asian Elephants', the workshop will focus on educating and training forestry personnel, community leaders and other stakeholders who are directly or indirectly involved in human–elephant related issues.

The participants will be taught how to use educational materials on human–elephant co-existence through exercises, games, dramas and stories. They will be provided elephant etiquette booklets, elephant packet items consisting of friendship band, masks, finger puppets, placards and stickers in both English and Dzongkha …

The stories are a necessary escape and they help to soften our landing. After a while I come to realise that the sweet melancholy I feel is not really for Bhutan as it is, so much as Bhutan the way it wants to be – spiritual, democratic, inclusive and happy, serviced by a media that reflects all that back to its people. It's an impossible ideal, but that doesn't matter. I'm happy that somewhere in the world they've set the bar so high.

EPILOGUE

A Nation with Many Voices

Bhutan stays with me, and I find my thoughts wandering to that hidden corner of the world where they are doing much the same things as me, just very differently. I read *Bhutan Observer*'s e-edition each Friday and stay in touch with Phuntsho by email, keeping up with the newspaper's ongoing struggles. In October 2011 she writes that the situation has become critical. Government advertising has dropped and they have no choice but to sack 28 of the 57 staff and close three of the four rural bureaus. She is devastated. I'm on the last leg of my doctoral thesis on the media in Bhutan and need to update my research, so I persuade my university to fund a return trip and convince my family that they can do without me for three weeks.

I arrive in Thimphu to find a severely diminished *Bhutan Observer.* Phuntsho has taken over as chief executive officer and Tenzin has moved full-time into another family business. The newspaper has sublet three-quarters of its office space and the remaining 29 staff members are squashed into a couple of rooms. Over tea, biscuits and the clanging sounds of a funeral *puja* nearby, Phuntsho and Needrup explain the perilous state of the private newspaper industry. Six new newspapers have launched, along with three colour magazines. One magazine is dedicated to Bhutanese film, an industry that is thriving. Another magazine is aimed at women. The third is a news magazine, which published a few editions but hasn't been seen since. It is a staggering number of publications in a country with few readers.

Phuntsho says a series of foreign consultants have told the government that diversity of the press is crucial for democracy, so small independent players are to be encouraged. As a result, the government has waived their initial requirement that newspapers be published in both Dzongkha and English, and distributed nationally. It seems that anyone with a laptop and an idea can now get a newspaper licence and then a share of government advertising.

'These foreign experts have no understanding of the ground realities,' says Phuntsho. She's not bitter, she explains, just tired. For five years she's been battling with committees, government departments and just about everybody else to make them understand why good Bhutanese newspapers are needed. Instead, newspapers are increasing in number and declining in quality. It's a bleak picture.

Facebook, on the other hand, is blossoming into a dynamic forum for public issues. There are pages to debate the contentious tobacco act, as well as campaign for the release of a monk jailed for possessing Nu.120 (A$3.30) worth of tobacco. There are pages to expose corruption, advertise jobs, showcase photography, discuss Thimphu street fashion, promote vegetarianism (its motto – 'peace, love and spinach'), cheer on their Olympic archery team and swap recipes. The King's Facebook page is easily the most popular Bhutanese page, with over 100,000 'likes', and following not far behind is that of his new bride, Jetsun Pema.

In many ways Facebook was tailor-made for the Bhutanese. As an oral culture with strong family and village networks, they are used to getting things done via the people they know. The nature of Facebook, creating webs of connections and a chatty, social forum, is a perfect fit. With 55,000 users in Bhutan, it already has six times the readership of *Kuensel*.

During my visit the government switches on its Indian-funded Nu.537 million (A$14.7 million) fibre optic network connecting all 20 *dzongkhags* (regions) and I get a glimpse into the future. The government has established 100 community cyber centres to bring the internet to people all across the mountainous country. Eventually there will be 185. Each is equipped with at least one desktop computer, printer and photocopier, and will be staffed by a computer-literate Bhutan Post employee. The plan is that in a few years no-one in Bhutan will be more than one day's walk from a cyber centre. No longer will rural people have to travel to Thimphu to do their banking, pay telephone bills, apply for business licences, seek permits to cut timber, register births and deaths, and more. These community centres will connect them to all the government services as well as to news, blogs, Wikipedia, Facebook, and each other. As rural voices join this new public space, much of Phuntsho's vision for a place where Bhutanese voices tell Bhutanese stories may yet be realised – just not in her newspaper.

I visit the Opposition leader Tshering Tobgay, who continues to lead the way into this brave new world of digital media. In 2009 his blog, one of the first in the country, averaged around 300 hits a day. Two years later he gets up to 10,000 hits a day. When an earthquake devastated Bhutan, he visited remote villages and posted photos of damaged houses to his 1,000-plus Twitter followers. He is a one-man publishing empire. Dressed in a crisply pleated *gho*, with a shiny silver MacBook closed on his desk and the latest iPhone by his briefcase, he represents the face of modern Bhutan.

When I ask him about the state of the private newspapers, he says he doesn't care. He only reads *Kuensel,* and then only because he feels he has to.

'Most of the others I skim. I'm not one of these old men who sit back and read every story in a newspaper. It's not because I am busy. It's because I'm lazy. I like to lie back on the couch and watch

TV … This is what the newspapers have to compete with. This is the reality,' he says with a laugh.

Tshering, 46, is highly educated and literate, with a Bachelor of Science in Engineering from the University of Pittsburgh and a Master in Public Administration from Harvard, but he just doesn't like newspapers. He finds them irrelevant.

I track down Dolma and she suggests we meet at a trendy new internet cafe in the main street. Her daughters, whom she brings with her, are growing into articulate, independent young women, yet it is Dolma who is most changed. While the girls update their Facebook pages, Dolma tells me Arjun has gone for good. But even better than that, she says with a proud smile, is her new legal status. She withdraws from her handbag stamped citizenship papers and a new bankbook. Two years ago she often seemed to be cowering, as if trying to take up less space. Today she sits easily in this modern cafe, every inch an equal to the rest of the crowd. She confidently orders a cappuccino and a piece of banana cake – in honour of Mal, she says, who taught her how to make it.

There is something very convivial about being able to fly in and immerse myself in what is happening here in Thimphu. People drop in and out of the newspaper office, staying for tea and gossip. There are new babies to meet and relationship updates. Sydney's depressing nightly news, with its emphasis on conflict, violence and money, feels a long, long way away. My visit ends all too soon and Phuntsho sends me home laden with gifts for the family, each one uniquely Bhutanese. I promise that next time I come I will bring her something specifically Australian.

Back in Sydney, I finish my thesis, quote the Fifth King in my graduation speech and continue to follow what is happening in Bhutan. Phuntsho's emails become increasingly gloomy. I subscribe to the e-edition of *Kuensel* and follow Bhutan's news via Twitter and Facebook. An anonymous website starts up: *Bhutanomics* is ferociously anti-government, and trying to unmask whoever is behind it becomes a hot topic on social media. The Opposition leader? Disgruntled journalists? In the lead-up to the July 2013 election, dozens of Twitter accounts spring up criticising the government, which is slow to catch on to this new phenomenon. For the 45,000 tweets that criticise them, the government responds with just 615 tweets. Tshering Tobgay manages 3,676 tweets along with posts on his Facebook page and blog. In this virtual space, at least, he is able to set the agenda. Not everyone is in on these conversations, but it doesn't matter. With strong family networks and widespread mobile-phone coverage, what is discussed in Thimphu spreads out to families in villages and beyond.

It becomes obvious even from 10,000 miles away that the liveliest public discussions are not in *Kuensel* or *Bhutan Observer* but online. On 13 July 2013, Mal and I, sitting in our lounge room in Sydney, follow the Bhutanese elections on Twitter. Seat by seat, the government falls. It is a landslide that no-one had predicted. Tshering Tobgay's party wins 32 seats and the incumbent party just 15. For days afterwards the country seems to be in shock. *We just voted out our first government.* How much of that result was due to social media, I wonder?

A year later I get further leave from my family and return to Bhutan to investigate how social media is working in the country. I email Phuntsho to tell her I'm coming. I've had three and a half years to think of a gift that will appeal to a Bhutanese media mogul who wants little beyond an end to suffering for all beings, but is quite partial to chilli and a chewy lump of dried pork rind. At the airport tourist shop, I find lurid packets covered in Australian flags that contain spicy kangaroo, emu and crocodile 'jerky'. They just about scream *Aussie, Aussie, Aussie, Oi, Oi, Oi.* Perfect!

At the airport Phuntsho is in a summer *kira* and greets me with a huge smile. We haven't made it out of the car park before she tells me sombre news. Next week she will close *Bhutan Observer.* It's time, she says. They haven't printed for a year, moving totally online to cut costs. It was intended as a temporary measure till income improved, but they have accepted that conditions for the print media can only get worse.

Thimphu now has an incredible 12 newspapers, and of the 11 owned privately, any of them could close at any time. Three newspapers haven't paid their staff for months. Some just print when they get advertising. Only *Kuensel* is doing okay, still getting half of the government's advertising. *Bhutan Observer* has managed to keep its webpage afloat because Needrup won the contract to publish Druk Air's in-flight magazine, *Tashi Delek*. But Phuntsho tells me that Needrup has just handed in his resignation. It was the catalyst she needed, she says, and now she is working up the courage to tell the last four loyal staff. Rabi, just back from Perth with his newly minted Master of Journalism, will take over editing *Tashi Delek*. Tenzin will find jobs for the other staff in his hardware business. And that, says Phuntsho, will be it for *Bhutan Observer.*

I feel a rush of emotions but Phuntsho smiles serenely, steering her little white Maruti around hair-raising bends. I marvel at her equanimity. She has been pushing this huge rock uphill for eight years. And now that's it? She shrugs. Her children are both healthy and doing well at school. She and Tenzin are happy. She has all her sisters around her. Life is good. She needs to recognise that and let go. It's a lesson for her in the Buddhist notion of impermanence. 'We could all be dead tomorrow,' she says, which I think is meant to cheer me up.

In the *Bhutan Observer* office, I find Needrup is just as philosophical. He says this is his opportunity to finally have a go at writing a book. Being fluent in Dzongkha, he thinks he can get enough part-time translation work to pay the family's bills.

I wander around Thimphu looking for copies of all these new newspapers that have helped push *Bhutan Observer* over the edge. The largest bookstore, which sells all the major Indian and international newspapers, stocks only *Kuensel*. I find *Business Bhutan* and *The Bhutanese* in a grocery store, but both are a week old. The others are nowhere to be found.

I visit *Kuensel* to meet with the editor and the chief political reporter. Even though this newspaper, with its circulation of 6,000 to 7,000, will undoubtedly survive, the editor says the state of the private media saddens him. 'They are literally dying. Now we have no competition. From 2006 to 2008 was the best time. There was *Bhutan Times* and *Bhutan Observer*, then *Bhutan Today*. We used to get the other newspapers and compare their coverage with ours, see what stories they had covered that we hadn't. Now those journalists have just gone.'

We talk about the rise of social media as a forum for news. One *Kuensel* reporter has been assigned full-time to social media, to find stories for the newspaper as well as to spread their own stories further afield. As *Kuensel*'s political reporter says, social media is both a competitor and a source. She gets many story leads from Facebook as most MPs have their own pages, which they use to communicate with their constituents, trying out policy ideas and seeking feedback.

I talk to more people and it becomes clear that apart from newspaper journalists, Phuntsho and me, few care that private newspapers are dying. Most people say they never read them, so they won't miss them. Instead they keep referring me back to the internet and the many interesting Facebook pages and blogs. One name in particular keeps coming up. Passu.

Everyone in Bhutan with access to the internet knows Passang 'Passu' Tshering. He is a high school teacher from Wangdue Phodrang, a few hours east of Thimphu, and he writes a popular blog about things that matter to him, which often then come to matter to everybody else.

I'm in luck that it is school holidays and he is in Thimphu, so we arrange to meet.

Ten minutes with Passu is exhilarating. He speaks quickly, ideas tumbling out in a steady stream. Aged about 30, he is excited by all the possibilities of modern media, poking around to see what they can do. He launched 'B-Bay' on Facebook, which has 30,000 Bhutanese members all across the country selling everything from houses and cars to air tickets, laptops and *kiras*. Another success is his cyber 'park' at Bajothang High School, which provides students with internet access outside school hours. On weekends many of Wangdue Phodrang's youth can be found in Passu's park, on their laptops and mobile phones, finding material for assignments, uploading their own music videos to YouTube or catching up on Facebook. He has many more projects, including setting up a museum to rural life and a Wi-Fi book cafe, and he wants to write a series of children's books with Bhutanese heroes ... The list is endless.

Passu says the internet arrived in 1999 but took off in Bhutan only after Bhutanese started to join Facebook in significant numbers in 2006. It now has around 130,000 users, he says. Such is its importance that he speaks in terms of before and after Facebook.

Like Tshering Tobgay, Passu doesn't read newspapers. 'If something is important it will be on Facebook,' he says.

Passu's blog has become an influential forum and people pay attention to what he writes. *Bhutan Times* sometimes publishes an entire post as 'news'. When two illicit Bhutanese sex videos started to circulate, it took Passu to make it a public issue. One had been filmed through a hotel door peephole, and in the other a young Bhutanese woman clearly had no idea she was being filmed. Both appeared in Passu's Facebook feed. 'Everyone was talking about them, but the newspapers weren't writing anything,' says Passu. So he wrote a piece on his blog, chastising anyone who watched the videos, re-posted them or forwarded them by phone. His post had 25,000 hits.

'There was a huge reaction from people saying they wanted to do something but didn't know how,' he says. 'After my blog I noticed people started removing the videos from Facebook.'

Kuensel interviewed Passu about his blog post, as did popular radio DJ Namgay Zam, who then started an online petition on change.org calling for laws against the non-consensual distribution of sexual material. Bhutanese leaders signed up, including Dzongsar Khyentse Rinpoche and the electoral commissioner. Two months after Passu's post, the government called a high-level meeting to discuss strategies to deal with social-media porn.

Passu is the unofficial leader of the growing number of bloggers in Bhutan and he takes me to one of their semi-regular meet-ups at a bar in Thimphu. Bhutan's bloggers, or the ten that come drinking this evening, are passionate about their role in the media landscape. Some are former journalists without a job, others just experimenting with having a voice.

Forty-something Tshering Dorji from Paro says the internet has been a revelation to him. 'In my generation we were bullied by teachers at school. We couldn't speak up about our opinions. We didn't *know* you could write books. Now we can all have a voice.'

Tshering broke a major story about corruption at the Food Corporation of Bhutan, which has been followed up for investigation by the Anti-Corruption Commission.

Another blogger, Riku Dhan Subba, is a former *Bhutan Observer* journalist with a passion for social justice. His most popular post criticised late-night partying – and the rubbish left behind – at the foot of the massive new Buddha statue that sits high above Thimphu. Everybody in the city was complaining about it, but the TV and newspapers never mentioned it until Riku made it an issue on his blog. Riku likes the interaction with blog readers, saying that when he was writing for the newspaper he was never sure anyone read his stories.

The bloggers have created their own vibrant corner in Bhutan's growing media space, starting public discussions, exposing problems and reporting news. What they write about spreads via Facebook, Twitter, radio and word of mouth. The whisky flows and I leave them happily arguing about the sexual antics of Drukpa Kinley.

While I'm here I volunteer to take some workshops for Siok-Sian Pek-Dorji at the Bhutan Centre for Media and Democracy. I know they are doing clever things with young people and media, and this gives me a chance to see for myself. For the school holidays, Pek has brought together students and teachers from all over the country to attend ten-day programs on using modern media to be engaged citizens and help their communities. Pek wants them to go beyond the old news paradigm of exposing problems, instead empowering them also to find solutions. In one program she has partnered with UNICEF to teach the youth about 'community mapping'. In groups they learn to identify what makes communities strong, how to interview people, how to tell stories using photography and digital media, and how civic policies are made, and then they are set loose in Thimphu to find both problems and solutions. By 'mapping' these communities they discover that many issues can be solved at the local level by ordinary citizens.

One group tells me they want to tackle the problem of childhood obesity. I'm surprised. *Obesity?* 'Given all the walking you do, I wouldn't have thought that was such a problem …?' I venture. They laugh. They know from the internet that obesity is an issue in the West and they are teasing me. 'We don't have fat people like you do,' one says. In fact, the group is interested in the problems of street hawkers illegally selling vegetables on the main street. The hawkers can't afford to pay for stalls at the market but they clog up the footpath, upsetting shopkeepers. To remedy the situation, the students find a sympathetic company who will not only allow the hawkers to set up outside their front door, but also build them a canopy to protect them from rain.

Other groups in the program tackle issues such as buying local rather than imported food, changing a bus route to improve access for people living in a slum on the outskirts of town, and helping disabled people get from the hospital and across a busy road to the Memorial Chorten.

At the end of the ten days the groups present their results as short videos, which they will upload to YouTube and spread on social media for the benefit of other communities facing similar challenges. I sit with Phuntsho in the audience, feeling inspired. More than 60 per cent of the Bhutanese population is aged under 25, and while nearly 10 per cent of youth are unemployed – some of whom are clearly visible in the town square, high on cough medicine or worse – these shiny faces are their counterparts. Bright, engaged and ready to tackle the issues, big and small, facing their country. Phuntsho is equally moved. With her newspaper about to close, I can see her mind working furiously. 'This is very good,' she says. 'I must talk to Pek …'

Pek and Kinley invite me for dinner at their home. As secretary to the Minister of Information and Communications, it is Kinley's job to write the country's media policy. He has just returned from an international conference in Korea, and is thinking about ways in which social media fits within the framework of Gross National Happiness. He thinks many countries aren't recognising the cultural and spiritual possibilities of social media.

As an example of its potential, he tells me two stories. A few years ago he had trouble getting his two sons to join him at the Thimphu *tshechu* to watch the famous Black Hat dance. The boys thought it would be slow and boring until they found a video of it on YouTube. The clip started with a close-up on a spinning black hat, before zooming out to reveal the whole performance. The boys were entranced. It gave them a new perspective on their own culture.

Recently, the elder son returned from studying at Stanford University and went to visit his uncle, a yogi who was doing a lifetime retreat in a remote cave. Taking his mobile phone, the young man called up old film footage he had found at his American university of his uncle's Buddhist master. They watched it together, in his cave, high on a mountaintop. Again, it shows how this deeply spiritual country is using modern media to serve its own cultural practices.

But, Kinley says, for all its power, social media will never replace word of mouth for spreading news throughout Bhutan. It was his greatest competitor when he was editor of *Kuensel* and is still how most news travels. 'Even now, if you ask people *where do you hear things, how do you learn things?* they say *through my friend or family.* Word of mouth is very important now. We are largely an oral society.'

Kinley is unfussed about the state of newspapers. He believes there is only room for two or three and whichever are still standing in five years will be the winners. It's survival of the fittest.

The strong oral nature of the society works well with mobile phone technology. Instead of sending text messages, many prefer to use the app WeChat to record and then send short voice messages. This is cheaper than a phone call, and Phuntsho swaps voice messages with various sisters throughout the day. She says it's also very popular with monks, who record *pujas* and send them to each other.

I'm often amazed at the creative ways Bhutanese use their mobile phones. Although they were introduced only in 2003, nearly 93 per cent of households now own at least one. BBS and *Kuensel* regularly run stories about how the mobile phone has changed people's lives. The Ministry of Agriculture provides a daily recorded message giving updates of vegetable prices at markets across the country. Instead of driving for days only to find a glut of their particular crop, farmers can ring and find out where they will get the best price. *Kuensel* also reports that farmers no longer have to walk to neighbouring villages to pass on messages. They can call for urgent help when wild animals attack their crops, and the phone doubles as a handy torch.

While few can afford smartphones, a basic, black-and-white

Nokia can play Bhutanese movies stored on memory cards, and people transfer them to one another over Bluetooth. One farmer says he has watched 25 Bhutanese movies on his phone. Another has two Bhutanese movies and a few cartoons for his two-year-old son stored on a 2GB memory card in his Nokia phone.

One unforeseen consequence of the mobile phone is that it has brought an end to the rural practice of night-hunting. These days, the reporter notes wistfully, men and women call each other.

I finish my two-week visit feeling melancholy for *Bhutan Observer* and what could have been, but excited, even inspired, by the many ways the country is using other media. The mobile phone has been as revolutionary as I imagine the printing press must have been to 15th-century Europe. Facebook is similarly impressive, challenging all my preconceptions of what it means to be literate. Needrup uses it to keep in touch with his childhood friends in Mongar, a few days' travel away. Some of them didn't go beyond the equivalent of Grade 3 at their local primary school and can't read or write English or Dzongkha. They speak only their local dialect, Chocha Ngacha, which has no written form, but they know enough of the Roman alphabet to write it phonetically on Facebook.

The internet has created new public spaces where Bhutanese are debating government policies, praising their Kings, swapping second-hand goods, exposing corruption, challenging laws, arguing about Gross National Happiness and considering all the things that matter to them as citizens. Rural cyber centres and cheap mobile phones from China and India are extending these spaces to most corners of the country.

Eleven years after *The Guardian*'s story, it turns out TV didn't kill Shangri-La by introducing sex and crime to the society. Pek's latest research shows that Bhutanese are still more interested in what's happening inside their country than out. International sport, Korean pop music and Hindi soaps are popular, but the more local films and TV shows are made, the less foreign shows are watched. Pek's research reveals a dramatic decline in the consumption of international media, which correlates with an increase in Bhutanese content. Farmers aren't swapping *Terminator 3* by Bluetooth; they're swapping local films about Buddhist heroes – stories that demonstrate compassion and kindness, according to one farmer.

Newspapers haven't been a great success. And as much as I wanted *Bhutan Observer* to achieve all of Phuntsho's ambitions, I realise something else as I prepare to leave: perhaps they are better off without them. It's a strange position for me to arrive at. I love newspapers. My father was a print journalist and I've been a print journalist most of my working life. But by leapfrogging over the development stage of print, they also missed the stage where print capitalism created a business model for newspapers. Consumer advertising, much like newspapers themselves, is a foreign concept. Bhutan doesn't have billboards screaming 'Want longer lasting sex?' Shopfronts aren't adorned with signs promising 'Things go better with Coke'. Instead, the little advertising there is comes from government departments seeking tenders and aid organisations advising how to avoid flu, as well as warm felicitations to their Kings on their birthdays. Social media, the internet and blogs may well provide a public space for discussion about things that matter to Bhutanese without bringing the baggage of rampant consumerism.

The Bhutanese have a saying – *take the best of the West and leave the rest* – and that's what they're doing. They are creating a dynamic public space to serve a 21st-century democracy across all the modern platforms available. The people known as *drukpas,* in this once-hidden land they call Druk Yul, know the media experiences of other countries and want to do it differently, according to their own philosophy of Gross National Happiness. They are a nation with many voices – on the phone, radio, Facebook, TV, Twitter, blogs and more. As Kinley Dorji said: 'We Bhutanese love to talk.'

Acknowledgments

It was an extraordinary privilege to be in the Kingdom of Bhutan as it took its first steps as a democracy. The year spent working with *Bhutan Observer* challenged me both professionally and personally. The owners of the newspaper, Tenzin Wangdi and Phuntsho Wangmo, brought a dedication to benefiting their society that was, dare I say, outside my previous experience of media moguls. Their approach to applying the ideals of Gross National Happiness to their media business was truly inspiring.

I am grateful for the openness of editor-in-chief Needrup Zangpo and the rest of the newspaper staff, including Rabi Dahal, Tandin Pem, Wesel Wangmo, Metho Dema, Gopal Singh and Sushil Mishra.

Thank you to Dasho Kinley Dorji and Siok Sian Pek for their hospitality and sharing their knowledge of the media in Bhutan; Tshering Tashi for his help with history; Prime Minister Tshering Tobgay for his generous gift of time; Dasho Neten Zangmo, one of the most inspiring people I have had the good fortune to meet; Kay Kirby Dorji, a wonderfully wise woman; the erudite Vice Chancellor of Royal University of Bhutan, Dasho Pema Thinley; and the hard-working, compassionate Lama Shenpen.

Mal, Kathryn and I thoroughly enjoyed our time as part of the Tashi Pelkhil community, with wonderful neighbours Megan Ritchie and Thinley Dorji, and Hans van Noord and Cecile de Boer, who, along with their children, have become lifelong family friends. We also appreciated the camaraderie of Fiona and Dave Stiedl, Sally Warriner, Jesper and Miki Krebs, and the rest of the small expat community in Thimphu, who all have now dispersed to the four winds. May you all enjoy many more adventures. And sincere, heartfelt thanks to all the Bhutanese who touched our lives, both directly and indirectly, and showed us their Bhutan, in all its complicated glory.

In Australia, I thank my two thesis supervisors Dr Willa McDonald and Dr Catherine Simpson, for guiding me through the bewildering world of academia. They challenged me with intellectual rigour, but also with kindness and good humour. I am grateful to publisher Madonna Duffy for seeing merit in this book and also for putting me in the literary care of the very capable Ian See, a genius on structure and detail.

Thank you also to Australia's Honorary Consul for Bhutan, Catherine Harris, and her husband, David; and to Australia's special envoy to Bhutan, Tim Fischer.

And finally, to Dzongsar Khyentse Rinpoche, Mal Watson and Kathryn Avieson, I wouldn't know where to start. So just … thank you.

References

Chapter 3 ***Braying Donkeys***

32, line 19 Needrup Zangpo, 'The braying donkeys and barn managers', *Bhutan Observer*, 17 October 2008.

Chapter 4 ***Night-hunting***

35, line 23 Sonam Choden, letter to the editor, *Bhutan Times*, 28 September 2008.

36, line 28 Peky Samal, 'Watch out night-hunters', *Bhutan Times*, 24 September 2008.

38, line 15 Needrup Zangpo, 'Illegality of night-hunting', *Bhutan Observer*, 26 September 2008.

38, line 32 Tashi Dema, 'The dark side of night-hunting', *Kuensel*, 2 October 2008.

39, line 18 Needrup Zangpo, 'Defining night-hunting', *Bhutan Observer*, 3 October 2008.

Chapter 5 ***Tashi Pelkhil***

48, line 31 Dipika Chhetri, 'Now, who is a Dasho?', *Bhutan Today*, 20 February 2009.

Chapter 8 ***Happy, Happy, Happy***

68, line 26 Rabi Dahal, 'Ungar diary', *Bhutan Observer*, 13 February 2009.

71, line 7 Quoted in John Elliott, 'The modern path to enlightenment', *Financial Times*, 2 May 1987.

71, line 24 Karma Ura, *Explanation of GNH Index*, Centre of Bhutan Studies, 2008.

Chapter 12 ***The Myth of Shangri-La***

101, line 6 Mark Coddington, 'Islander's latest adventure takes him to Bhutan, world's happiest country', *The Grand Island Independent*, 30 May 2009.

101, line 15 Editorial, 'Coffee table Bhutan', *Bhutan Times*, 14 June 2009.

104, line 23 Tashi Dema, 'The Monpas of Trongsa are Monpas no more', *Kuensel*, 24 September 2008.

105, line 8 Dzongsar Khyentse Rinpoche, 'About Gross National Happiness', *Kuensel*, 9 May 2010.

106, line 4 Cathy Scott-Clark and Adrian Levy, 'Fast forward into trouble', *The Guardian*, 14 June 2003.

107, line 25 Siok Sian Pek-Dorji, *Media Impact Study 2003*, Ministry of Information and Communications, Royal Government of Bhutan, 2003.

108, line 15 William Langley, 'Profile: The King of Bhutan – The prince who brought satellite TV to Shangri-La', *The Telegraph*, 8 November 2008.

Chapter 14 ***A Victory for the Media***

121, line 9 Tim Fischer and Tshering Tashi, *Bold Bhutan Beckons*, CopyRight Publishing, 2008.

Chapter 15 ***Wooden Phalluses and Crooked Vaginas***

126, line 8 Quoted in Gopilal Acharya, 'Of phallus: an arcane symbol', *Kuensel*, 3 February 2003.

126, line 24 Noa Jones, press kit for *Travellers & Magicians*, produced for Zeitgeist Films, 2004.

128, line 20 Rabi Dahal, 'Crooked female genitalia and the legend that straightened things out', *Bhutan Observer*, 9 January 2009.

Chapter 18 ***Two Remarkable Women***

155, line 24 Pushkar Chhetri, 'Corruption, not a shame', *Bhutan Observer*, 19 June 2009.

157, line 3 'Dasho Neten Zangmo receives red scarf', *Kuensel*, 27 December 2008.

160, line 10 Metho Dema, 'The happy little home', *Bhutan Observer*, 13 July 2009.

Chapter 19 ***Forbidden Topics***

162, line 13 Samten Yeshi, 'A seemingly motiveless murder', *Kuensel*, 28 March 2009.

164, line 20 Quoted in Vishal Arora, 'Religious conversion worst form of "intolerance"', *Compass Direct News*, 13 April 2011.

Chapter 21 ***The Outside World***

188, line 19 Jigmi Y Thinley, statement at the 63rd Session of the General Assembly of the United Nations, 26 September 2008.

Chapter 22 ***Floods of Change***

195, line 26 Editorial, 'Down by the riverside', *Kuensel*, 3 August 2009.

196, line 17 Needrup Zangpo, 'A lesson on disaster', *Bhutan Observer*, 3 August 2009.

Chapter 23 ***Getting Along with Elephants***

208, line 1 Eshori Gurung, 'First elephant awareness workshop', *Bhutan Observer*, 6 March 2010.

PEACEMONGERS
Barry Hill

In his first major prose work since 2002's *Broken Song*, Barry Hill has written a monumental epic – a travel book, a history book, a peace book. His odyssey begins with a pilgrimage to Bodh Gaya in India, where the Buddha received enlightenment, and ends after he reaches Nagasaki, Japan, in the aftermath of its atomic bomb.

His travelling is imbued with the life and ideas of India's greatest artist and intellectual, Rabindranath Tagore, along with that of Gandhi. Hill then travels, like Tagore, in Japan, and meditates on its militarist turn, its warmongering Buddhism and the Tokyo War Crimes Trial, with its riddled post-colonial legacy. As he muses on his own capacity for inner-disarmament, Hill also has his late father with him, a union man and Australian peace activist, whose dated left-humanism may not be enough for the wars and ruins the West has recently created.

The discourse of this incredible work – poetic, mobile, ambivalent – seeks to be an antidote to the political impotence of progressive thought over the last decade. But *Peacemongers* does not peddle hope, and when it sights hope it tends to be as an epiphany, as it was with Tagore.

> 'Barry Hill is blessed with the gifts of a fine essayist, historian, philosopher and poet. I know of no other writer who honours them with such audacious yet disciplined originality.'
>
> Raimond Gaita

> '*Peacemongers* is not only a compelling literary quest, but a book of ethics for the coming times.'
>
> Justin Clemens

UQP

ISBN 978 0 7022 5325 6

THE PROMISE OF ICELAND
Kári Gíslason

In 1990, at the age of seventeen, Kári Gíslason travelled to Iceland, the land of his birth, and arranged to meet his father. What he found was not what he expected.

Born from a secret liaison between his British mother and Icelandic father, Kári moved regularly between Iceland, England and Australia. He grew up aware of who his father was, but understood his mother had promised never to reveal his father's identity. It was a promise his father would also ask him to keep.

A decade later, Kári made the decision to break that promise, and he contacted his half-siblings, who knew nothing of his existence. What led him to this decision and what followed makes for a heartfelt and riveting journey traversing landscapes, time and memory, of one man's search for a sense of belonging.

> 'Gorgeously told ... a quietly moving and affecting memoir ... Highly recommended.'
>
> Krissy Kneen, *Avid Reader*

> '[A] memorable, finely crafted book.'
>
> *The Age*

> 'A deeply charming account of displacement, of not really knowing where you come from and how that makes it difficult to know where you belong.'
>
> *The Sunday Mail*

> 'A powerful memoir about landscape and identity.'
>
> *The Advertiser*

UQP

ISBN 978 0 7022 3582 2

CPSIA information can be obtained at www.ICGtesting.com
Printed in the USA
LVOW01s0009170715

446472LV00003B/5/P